TEACH
ME
TO
TEACH

TEACH
ME
TO
TEACH

Dorothy G. Swain

JUDSON PRESS®
VALLEY FORGE

TEACH ME TO TEACH
Copyright © 1964
The Judson Press
Valley Forge, Pa.
Sixth Printing, 1979

Library of Congress Catalog Card No. 64-13125

International Standard Book No. 0-8170-0316-9

The name JUDSON PRESS is registered as a trademark in the U.S. Patent Office.

PRINTED IN THE U.S.A. ⊕

TEACH ME TO TEACH . . .

CONTENTS

BY WAY OF INTRODUCTION

In the teaching process, an open door is set before the learner. The teacher, standing with the learner at this door, calls attention to fields of knowledge and experience which lie beyond — inviting exploration and discovery. If the learner is sufficiently challenged, and so chooses, he crosses the threshold to find these treasures and to claim them.

In this book, which is quite different from the usual leadership education text, we meet a group of church school teachers who have just such a door open before them. They come from varying backgrounds and experiences, each with specific problems and needs he hopes can be met in the local leadership training school he is attending. Under the guidance of Mr. Johnson, an experienced and understanding leader, these teachers are helped to find answers to many of their questions, and are challenged to explore new ways of making their teaching more effective and relevant.

Come now and join this group of learning teachers. Meet Ralph Moody, Kate Powell, Bert Smith, Bruz Hendricks, Frances Lane, and others of this class as they discuss experiences in church school teaching. Consider along with them what the vocation of Christian teaching involves, and learn how you, too, may become a more effective teacher.

The door is set before you. The decision to step forward and to explore the vast world of Christian teaching is left with you.

MEET SOME MEMBERS OF THE
CHURCH SCHOOL TEACHERS'
LEADERSHIP TRAINING CLASS

Ralph Moody — the unwilling teacher of a fifth grade class.

Bert Smith — the satisfied teacher of the adult class which has met regularly for years in the Tower Room.

Kate Powell — the puzzled teacher of primary children, frustrated by Billy and Paul.

Bruz Hendricks — a pre-law student who agreed to teach the high school class provided "it takes no time but Sunday mornings."

Frances Lane — the conscientious ex-English teacher who now has a class of seventh graders, with Todd as a standout.

Norma Newcomb — the uneasy teacher of a junior high class.

Mary Bliss — a teacher of juniors whose classes "are always good."

Mr. Johnson — leader and guide of the leadership class.

1

. . . THROUGH
FACING UP TO MYSELF
AS TEACHER

RALPH MOODY WAS TIRED AND DISCOURAGED. HIS SUNDAY church school class of fifth graders had just left the room noisily. He thought back over the session. What had been accomplished? Pete had been so vocal that Ralph had had to ask him to keep quiet. Alice, on the other hand, had sat sullenly through the period, saying nothing. Sam and Doug had got into a scuffle over who would sit in the newest chair in the room. Only Henry had seemed cooperative; yet Ralph had an uncomfortable feeling that the rest of the class disliked him. Ralph, a government accountant on weekdays, was used to orderliness and precision. A scene such as that which he had just witnessed bore no resemblance to his weekday pattern of life. The lesson today had been "Jesus' Trip to the Temple." Henry alone had shown interest. "I shouldn't have agreed to take this class," he thought. "I don't know how to teach. But what could I say when the committee insisted?"

In the Tower Room, Bert Smith had concluded his weekly lesson with the adults of the church. The period left him inspired, as usual. Bert Smith had taught many years. On weekdays he operated the Flower Mart in the

11

center of town and was considered an expert in floral arrangements. On Sundays he held forth in the Tower Room. Stimulated by the class's attentiveness, he lectured for the full hour, and only severe illness kept him from his group of faithfuls. "It is my way to serve the Lord," he would explain, "and I don't want to miss one opportunity."

Kate Powell was on her way home from church when she caught sight of Billy and Paul, two of the children in her primary class. Billy had taken Paul's hat and thrown it into the street. Paul had gone after it, caught up with the fleeing Billy, and was pounding him. "Why *does* Billy pick on Paul?" Kate puzzled. "And it was Billy who knew all the answers for our lesson today on 'Love Your Neighbor.' Where have I failed?"

The high school class had had a lively discussion this morning, and Bruz Hendricks, the teacher, was inwardly elated. They were working on "Ideas of God" at Mary's suggestion; Mary, Ted, and Sue — all senior honor students at the high school — had carried the discussion. Bruz now marked the attendance cards to turn in to the church school secretary. He noted idly that George, Howie, and Ross had been absent for several weeks. He doubted if any had missed them; sophomores, they had never entered into the discussion with the others and usually either sat a bit aloof or sparred with each other in the back row. Still glowing over the last point he and Sue had argued before the class session ended, Bruz — a pre-law student — started for home over his usual route via South Main Street. In front of George's house were his three truants — grease-covered as they worked on a hot rod. "So that's what they were up to!" Bruz thought. "I'll have to get after them for missing class."

Frances Lane was preparing Sunday dinner when her husband asked her the usual question, "Well, how was your class today?" He knew that Frances had many uncertainties about her group of junior highs. "I wish I knew!" she replied. "The session took such an unexpected turn when Todd began firing irrelevant questions. We never did complete the lesson the way I'd planned it. We were reviewing 'Jesus' Return to Nazareth,' and I was planning to have them make a play out of it (they love plays), when out of the blue, Todd asked, 'Why do people keep Lent?' After we had handled that question he had another ready, 'Why do people eat fish on Friday?' By that time Joan was puzzling aloud on how Jesus could go forty days without food. The class period ended before we had accomplished anything." Mr. Lane looked fondly at his wife; she seemed exhausted after her ordeal with the seventh graders. "Why do you keep on teaching?" he asked. "Your weekends would be so much pleasanter, and you say yourself that you cannot see that you are accomplishing anything. I think it's time to give up the class."

When the area leadership training school for church school teachers was announced, it was not surprising that Ralph Moody, Kate Powell, and Frances Lane enrolled at once. Bert Smith, however, was reluctant to attend. "I've taught for years," he said. "Why should I go to such a class?" Bruz Hendricks, too, was slow to respond when the general superintendent told him about the class. "I'm busy at college during the week," he argued, "and give all the time I can to my church school class by coming on Sunday morning. I don't need to spend six nights learning how to teach. All a teacher needs to do is to throw out an idea and let the kids bite into it; I like that method of teaching and I'm sure they all like it, too. We have great discussions." It took much persuasion to get Bert Smith and Bruz to attend the leaders' class, but they finally consented to go to the first session "just to see what it was like." And so they went.

They joined men and women from several churches in the area enrolled in the course on teaching at the leadership school. Session One was called "Why Teach?" Bert Smith sat stiffly in the circle as introductions were made. He was waiting for the lecture to begin, when they would get down to business. Frances Lane had her pencil and notebook ready, remarking to her neighbor, "I need every bit of help I can get!" Bruz looked amused as he studied the widely differing group of teachers about him, some of them so earnest. Ralph Moody was hoping someone would let him tell about his troubles with the fifth grade.

Why teach?

"We have three major concerns tonight," the leader, Mr. Johnson, said after people had gotten acquainted. "This first evening we are to look into three questions which may appear to have obvious answers. Since this is a large group, to make discussion easier and more profitable, we are now going to number off into small groups of six each. In the small groups we will handle the first two of the three questions I am going to state. We will discuss the third question as a total group later. Each small group will discuss these first two questions for ten minutes and then bring back findings to share with the entire group. Each group should select a secretary to keep a record of what its findings are. These are the questions:

1. *Why are you teaching?*
2. *Why do your pupils attend?*
3. *What are the signs of a good class?*

In group A where Ralph Moody was assigned, Ralph opened the discussion with an honest confession. "I'll tell you why *I* am teaching. My wife was on the recruiting committee. She got down to the end of the list with no results, and my name was the last one on it. You can bet I won't be teaching next year, though." Everyone laughed at his frankness. The secretary recorded Ralph's reason.

Kate Powell was also in group A. "I suppose my reason

for teaching may not be the best, but I am teaching this year out of gratitude for all the years of teaching which others have given to the teaching of *my* children. I am free to teach, now that the children are older, and so I felt it was time to do my round of duty in the church school." The secretary recorded her remarks.

Bert Smith was in group B. He was a bit impatient with the reasons for teaching which others were giving, such as:

"The church needs teachers and I felt duty-bound."

"I've always loved boys and girls."

"I'm so disturbed at the juvenile delinquency problem. We must do something to conquer it and I think the church school is the place to start. Don't statistics say that children who go to Sunday school seldom end in court?"

Bert could stand it no longer. "*I* teach," he said, "because the Bible says we must teach. 'Go and teach,' it says. That means that we should be teaching the Bible, and that's what I aim to do. I explain it, and my class listens. We've been doing it that way for a dozen years."

"How is the attendance in your class?" asked Norma Newcomb, a newcomer in the community.

"We keep the same number year in and year out," Bert boasted.

Frances Lane and Bruz Hendricks were in group C. Frances' face was puckered in deep thought as the others voiced their reasons for teaching. Bruz was quite frank in giving his reason:

"High school age boys and girls like to have someone who talks their language. When I was asked to teach, I said I'd do it so long as it didn't take any of my time but Sunday morning. I usually go to class with this question, 'What do you want to discuss today?' There are a couple in the group who bring in deep subjects, so we've been on these."

"I don't quite know how to put my reason into words," Frances Lane said slowly. "I want the children to acquire a faith that is real. If only I could make the Bible come alive and be meaningful to them, so they will *want* to read it! Once in awhile I think I've done it, then someone says something that makes me wonder if I have been a complete failure."

The others nodded sympathetically.

Group A was now discussing question two. Ralph Moody was the first to respond again. "Why do my pupils come? That's a good question! I've asked that question myself, lots of times. Maybe one or two come because they want to, but I think all the rest come because their parents make them!"

Why do pupils attend?

There was general agreement. Kate Powell spoke up then. "I try to make my lessons so interesting that the children will want to come. But this takes such a lot of planning! I just don't have time for it. And besides, what interests one, doesn't interest another!"

Bert Smith was holding forth in group B. "Why do people come to Sunday school? Because they want to learn, of course. That's why my adults come. You should see their faces when I explain a verse to them."

"That does not sound much like my junior highs," Mrs. Newcomb commented. "I do believe all they come for is to see each other. You'd think no one else existed in their world." A fellow junior high teacher laughed in agreement.

Bruz looked somewhat smug as group C reached question two. "My class comes because they get a chance to discuss what they are interested in. Just give a group a subject they like, and they'll come."

Frances Lane was deep in thought again as the question was put to her. "I wish I knew how to get my pupils to come for the right motive — to learn about God. Once in awhile, I think maybe they do, but they cover this up with a front. I was planning to make my lesson interesting a few Sundays ago by having them dramatize Jesus' return to Nazareth. Instead, one of the boys got us off the sub-

ject, discussing some of his questions about other faiths.
Oddly, for the first time in weeks, I think the whole group
listened. Perhaps they were questions the others had been
wondering about, too. I wish I knew how to channel what
interests they have; I hope I will find out in this class."

When the three small groups reassembled as a total
group at the end of ten minutes, Mr. Johnson said he
wished to reverse the order of the dis-
cussion questions and begin with ques-   **What is a**
tion three, "What are the signs of a   **good class?**
good class?"

Mary Bliss, a member of the church in which the leadership school was being held, leaned forward to speak. As
she did so, a woman from this same church turned to her
neighbor and whispered loudly, "Mary's a wonderful
teacher. You should see her classes!" Aloud, she said,
"Describe your classes, Mary. They're *good!*"

Mary spoke with assurance. "Well, I always have been
proud of my junior boys and girls. We cover our quarter-
lies each time and I never have discipline problems — or
noise. . . ." She gave a meaningful look toward the circle.

"I know what you mean," a man from North Church
replied. "I feel I have a good class too. We got rid of
the troublemakers and now I have six nice, cooperative
fourth graders."

Mr. Johnson repeated the question. "What do you all
think are the signs of a good class? You hear teachers
use this description frequently. In other words, what do
you set as your goal in teaching? What do you mean when
you say 'We had a good class today'?"

"They're *quiet!*" Ralph Moody laughed as he said this.
"So my class isn't good."

"They practice what they learn," added Kate Powell,
also laughing. "That lets my class out, too."

"They listen well, and want to learn," Bert Smith said,
with finality. "My adults make such a good class."

"It is possible to cover the lesson each week, the way *we* do." This came from Mary Bliss.

"Maybe it is a good class if pupils air the problems and questions on their minds?" suggested Frances Lane.

"Yes, that's right," Bruz nodded in her direction. "There is opportunity for debate."

"What do *you* think is a good class, Mr. Johnson?" Norma Newcomb asked. "These sound superficial to me."

"Let me define my idea of a good class by asking some questions," he countered. "Now first of all, let us examine the idea of a quiet, docile class which some of you have implied. Is this what we really want? How many of you have ever sat through a teaching session in which you merely listened passively to the teacher?"

1) Active involvement

Bruz laughed. "I did that in Economics 314 last year at college. It is a subject I do not like and never understood, but it was required as a part of my course. The professor used words I needed a dictionary to understand. It was impossible for me to ask him questions — I didn't know enough to ask any! So, since I understood so little, I got into the habit of daydreaming during the class."

"Would you say, then, Bruz, that a docile class may be the sign of a passive class, one that is disinterested in the subject matter, or lacks the vocabulary to understand what is going on in the classroom? That they sit quietly only because they are bored, or afraid to ask questions?"

"That's the way *I* felt in Economics 314."

"Does that mean that a class should be *noisy?*" Ralph Moody looked surprised. "Mine must be perfect then!"

Frances Lane replied to this comment. "When I took education courses at the University, I was taught that there is a noise called the 'hum of busyness' which is permissible because it is purposeful noise. I mean by that, something like a committee working together on a project and talking quietly about it as they work."

"That's not the way *my* class makes noise," Ralph Moody commented. "Their noise comes from arguments."

"There certainly are different kinds of noise, Ralph," Mr. Johnson answered. "Some noise hinders learning, but there is a kind that exhibits good teaching — purposeful, interested. Sometimes this is shown by spontaneous questions coming from the group."

Bert Smith was looking concerned. "Are you people implying that a class that listens, as mine does, is not a good class?"

"You yourself will have to be the judge," Mr. Johnson replied. "A teacher has to have a listening ear himself, constantly listening for what he can detect. Are there signs of real thinking and growth going on within the group? Or have you a case of Bruz and Economics 314? We're going to discuss evaluation at a later session of this class when we mention ways to detect how much is being taught." He paused, then said, "I think we should put a record of our findings on the chalkboard. Would someone volunteer to do this?" Kate Powell volunteered. She wrote:

2) Continuous evaluation by the teacher

SIGNS OF A GOOD CLASS

1. Busyness, alertness, active involvement, a thinking group

2. Continuous evaluation by the teacher

"I think a class that will discuss is a good class," Bruz said. "I have three pupils who love to discuss."

"How many do you have in your total class," asked Mr. Johnson.

"Fourteen," Bruz replied, "but they don't all come."

"My class will not discuss at all — at least, they will not discuss anything I want them to!" complained Norma Newcomb.

"Neither will mine," Ralph Moody echoed.

"What if one person dominates the discussion? That's what happened in my class last year," one of the men spoke for the first time.

"We will spend more time on this at a later session," Mr. Johnson said, "but let it be said right now, discussion can be meaningless, or very meaningful. If it is *creative*, it causes a pupil to use the ideas he already has as a foundation or a steppingstone to new and better ideas. You can call a discussion good when it meets this test. Also, its value comes when *everyone* is involved, not just a handful who like to hear themselves talk."

3) Creative discussion involving everyone

Bruz was taking this idea to heart. "But how could I ever get George or Ross or Howie to talk? I don't think they even care about what we're discussing."

On the list, Kate Powell was adding:

3. Creative discussion that involves everyone

Mary Bliss had not spoken for a long time. Obviously she had been doing some thinking. Now she spoke: "My daughter has been in a day school where a new boy has entered who has a speech defect. She said the pupils laughed at him the first day. Then I noted that she became much concerned about him, lest his feelings get hurt by the possible rudeness of the group. I have overheard her and her friends discussing his situation and the concern they felt toward him. One day I asked her if the classmates still laughed at him. She looked horrified. 'Oh no, Mother,' she replied, 'we're all trying to encourage him to speak without making mistakes. And, honestly, he is doing so much better! We almost cheer each time he succeeds.' Would we say that this is a good class if those children appreciate and seek to encourage and undergird that boy the way they do?"

4) Appreciation of worth and acceptance

"It sounds like an excellent situation to me," Mr. Johnson responded, "appreciating the worth of each member and being aware of his needs. How many of us can say this undergirding is going on in our church school classes? Is the 'different' child accepted by the others, in Christian love? Is there a redemptive spirit being put into practice?"

"What do you mean by 'different'?" Ralph Moody interrupted. "My Henry does not seem to fit in the class — the others don't like him. He's a nice kid, too. I've been wondering what could be done. . . ." his voice trailed off.

Kate Powell added to the list:

4. Appreciation of worth and acceptance in love

Then Frances Lane spoke. "Along this same line, I believe in the importance of knowing each pupil by name, as well as knowing his interests. I think anyone who teaches that God loves even the sparrow ought, as God's representative, to exemplify this love with individuals within his class."

5) Recognized as persons

"But supposing you have a large class like mine?" Mary Bliss asked. "The girls all look alike, and I have three whose first name is Linda. I'm always getting them mixed up."

"Just the same, I think it is important that we know our pupils as *persons* and be aware of their individual characteristics," Frances Lane insisted. "How otherwise can we teach about the importance of the individual in the sight of God?"

Mr. Johnson nodded in agreement. "Record it on the chalkboard, Mrs. Powell."

She wrote:

5. Recognized as persons

Under her breath, Mary Bliss was saying, "I never could remember names and faces."

Kate Powell was ready with another idea. "I think a

good class is one that is interested. That means the teacher has to beam the lesson to them in such a way that they *want* to learn. I think you call this getting them involved. Usually if one is involved in

6) Being involved

something, he gets interested, too."

"I have them looking up Bible references; isn't that involving them?" Ralph Moody looked around the circle for confirmation. "But they still act bored, or get restless while they wait for the slower ones to find the place."

Mr. Johnson had an answer, which he posed as a question. "Do you, Ralph, ever get impatient waiting for someone who does things more slowly than you, or does things just the same way, time after time? There are different ways of being involved, some more appealing than others."

7) Variety of methods

Kate Powell wrote:

6. Being involved in something one is interested in

7. Variety of method

"That still raises a problem for me," Ralph Moody persisted. "If my juniors have no interest in 'Jesus' Trip to the Temple,' how do I get them 'involved,' as you say?"

"That's a big subject, Ralph," Mr. Johnson replied, "and we will include it on our agenda before our sessions end. 'Motivation' is the technical word for this, and we will surely give it due consideration, for it underlies all teaching. Now is there anything else we should add to our list?"

8) Discipline stemming from Christian understanding and love

"Good discipline," the man from North Church said. "A good class has to have discipline. I had a boy who put tacks in the chairs. I told him he could get out and stay out. He hasn't been back. The same thing happened to the boy who came equipped with rubber bands. He hasn't showed up to bother our group for weeks. The rest of the group is good. You have to be firm and let them know who is boss."

"But what about that teaching of Jesus — that he came 'not to call the righteous, but sinners'?" Frances Lane looked concerned. "I think it is impossible to teach an unruly class, but I also think it is the job of us teachers to try to understand that kind of boy and to include him."

Mr. Johnson continued this line of thought. "Here is one place where the Christian teacher has a particular responsibility. Naturally he must recognize that misbehavior stems from a cause and try to root out such causes as he can. But he has also the responsibility and the opportunity to show redemptive love at the very point where it may be the most difficult. This is the message of the gospel, and pupils must see it in practice as well as in print."

Kate Powell added to the list:

> 8. *Discipline stemming from Christian understanding and love*

No one spoke for a few moments; all were reviewing the items on the list.

Norma Newcomb was the first to speak. "When I look at that list, I am scared. I realize all the requirements I have never met!"

"I am not sure I ever could!" Frances Lane added. "How can anyone?"

Humility in the light of the teaching task

"I must admit I feel better to discover that there are others who feel as inadequate as I do," Kate Powell spoke up. "I have felt I should be a perfect teacher, but that instead I am a complete failure."

Frances Lane hesitated, then continued. "I am almost ashamed — and afraid — to admit this, but I had a boy quit my class for seemingly no reason at all. I thought he was one of my most cooperative students — and suddenly he dropped out of my class. I could never find out why.

There is nothing like an experience of this kind to make you realize how you have failed." She hesitated, then added, "It hurt my pride, too!"

Mr. Johnson filled in what promised to be an awkward moment. "Mrs. Lane, I agree there is nothing which can hurt one's pride more than an experience like yours. Teaching can be very humbling. But I think I can read something deeper in your unhappiness. The church school teacher knows he has a vital mission to perform, and if he is honest, he views an experience like yours as a betrayal of the trust given him by God. He feels that he has been commissioned by God and that somehow, through his own human blundering, a child has been alienated from the very source of supply which he needs to foster his relationship with God. I used to find myself, as I reviewed classroom experiences, often quoting from Sill's poem, which I remember learning in college several years ago:

> *These clumsy feet, still in the mire,*
> *Go crushing blossoms without end;*
> *These hard, well-meaning hands we thrust*
> *Among the heart-strings of a friend.*
>
> *The ill-timed truth we might have kept —*
> *Who knows how sharp it pierced and stung?*
> *The word we had not sense to say —*
> *Who knows how grandly it had rung?*[1]

Who of us has not blunderingly caused some foot to turn away from the very message and agency which we represent? We lacked tact with the sensitive. We have nullified by our methods the very things we said with our lips. We have been teaching in a mass-production style, instead of for the individual person with his particular needs. We have taught in a way pleasing to ourselves, but not meet-

[1] "The Fool's Prayer," by Edward Rowland Sill. Boston: Houghton Mifflin Company. Used by permission.

ing the needs of the pupils. In short, we have neither listened to the voice of God, nor to the voice of man.

"I think we are at a proper starting point tonight. The Christian gospel itself begins with a sense of failure in our humanity and the recognition of our dependence upon God. In like manner we as teachers of the gospel should begin with an admission of human weakness and dependence upon divine help. Fortunately for us all, the gospel reminds us that God is seeking man in redemption; he has not left us marooned. This says something of hope to us as teachers and leaders, too. As Frances Lane has confessed, we fail. All of us fail. If each one of us is honest

The need of honest appraisal and admission of failure and inadequacy

with ourselves, we will have to confess that we have missed the mark, as one translation of the word 'sin' reads. Look at your pupils' *actual* attendance records against the *potential.* Have some members been lost by the wayside? Why? Look at the pattern of acceptance within your group — is Christian love prevailing? Why not? Look at the amount of active participation and involvement — what is your percentage and how deep is it? Look at each individual — how well has he been related to God and to his peers? What is your honest appraisal of this? Put your listening ear to work. These are but a few symptoms of weakness and failure in teaching. 'All have sinned.' 'Who can discern his errors? Clear thou me from hidden faults. Keep back thy servant also from presumptuous sins. . . .' "

The group was hushed. Mr. Johnson sensed a moment of worship was in order. Quietly he repeated the words familiar to them all:

Lord, speak to me, that I may speak
In living echoes of Thy tone;
As Thou hast sought, so let me seek
Thy erring children lost and lone.

O teach me, Lord, that I may teach
The precious things Thou dost impart;
And wing my words, that they may reach
The hidden depths of many a heart.

O fill me with Thy fulness, Lord,
Until my very heart o'erflow
In kindling thought and glowing word,
Thy love to tell, Thy praise to show.

O use me, Lord, use even me,
Just as Thou wilt, and when, and where;
Until Thy blessed face I see,
Thy rest, Thy joy, Thy glory share.

"Ours would be a discouraging situation if we ended our self-evaluation without the hope which this hymn describes. It is our reason for teaching and it is what makes teaching within the context of the Christian church *special*. Let's go back now to question one which you answered in your small groups: 'Why are you teaching?'"

No one spoke. Finally, Kate Powell said in a low voice, "I guess we all see how weak and inadequate the reasons were which we listed."

"We haven't the right motivation at all," Frances Lane added. "But where do we get it?"

"This subject is too big to handle tonight," Mr. Johnson replied. "It requires research and careful thinking. From what I overheard of your reasons for teaching, the motives sounded no different from those impelling any leader of any form of group work. Now the basic question is: Do you believe that as teachers, representing the Christian church, you have a responsibility that differs from that of a club leader?"

"Oh yes," everyone responded.

"How do you discover it?" Mr. Johnson persisted.

"In the Bible," Bert Smith answered with assurance.

"Does the Bible say anything specifically about teaching?" Frances Lane asked, with a puzzled look.

"Let's make that one phase of our research for next week, in addition to reading the first chapter in our text," Mr. Johnson suggested.

"Jesus was known as the Master Teacher; let's see how he did it," added Norma Newcomb.

"There ought to be a philosophy of teaching religion, the same as there is a philosophy of other things," Bruz commented.

"Trust our college student to see the importance of having a philosophy!" Mr. Johnson laughed. "Yes, Bruz, in Christian teaching we should examine our basic philosophy, for it does contribute to our motivation."

"I think we should look at the central message of the Scriptures," Bert Smith spoke out with firmness. "That gives us our reason for teaching."

"Are there volunteers to do research on these subjects, to enrich our study next week?" asked Mr. Johnson.

Frances Lane volunteered to look up what the Bible says about teaching. Norma Newcomb said she would look up material on Jesus, the Master Teacher. Bert Smith was unanimously elected to find the central message of the Bible.

Bruz was waiting for the question on a philosophy of Christian education. "That's my question," he said. "I'll take that one."

"I'm waiting for the committee that will deal with results of teaching," Ralph Moody remarked. "I like results — in accounting, and in everything else!"

Everyone laughed. "Don't worry, Ralph," Mr. Johnson was saying. "We all think results are important, and we'll remember to let you serve on that committee when we get to that subject."

It was late and adjournment was in order. "I'll see you all next week," Bruz called from the door. "We'll be here," the others called back.

STUDY QUESTIONS

1. Divide into small groups. Consider the questions:
   A. Why are you teaching?
   B. Why do your pupils attend?
   C. What are signs of a good class?
2. What is the unique responsibility of teachers within the Christian church?
3. Comment on the need and value of awareness as a part of the teacher's role. What does awareness include?
4. Begin making a list, to be carried through to the end of the book, of techniques and methods of teaching used by Mr. Johnson with his class during the six weeks.
5. How can a frank appraisal of one's weaknesses and failures in teaching become a wholesome experience?
6. Begin a discussion, which will continue throughout your study, on "The Role of Teacher — What Is It?"

2

. . . THROUGH
KNOWING WHY I TEACH

As USUAL, THIS HAD BEEN A BUSY WEEK FOR BRUZ. HE DID not forget his promise to investigate into the philosophy of Christian education; his problem was to find time to make the investigation. When he did settle down to it on the evening before the leadership class was to meet, he realized that he did not know where to look for the information he sought. As he sat at his desk, pondering, his eye lighted upon the pile of books stacked nearby. In the stack he saw the church school materials which the superintendent gave to him when he began teaching. At the time, Bruz had given them a quick glance, but had immediately rejected them because they looked wordy. Now, he began looking at them seriously.

He opened the teacher's book to the section called "Introduction." It was only recently that he had learned through college reading assignments the value of introductions to books. As he read, he was amazed at what he found. Here before him was a philosophy of Christian education spelled out! In the **Objective for Christian education** few moments which he had had during the past week to think about this subject, he had been baffled over what

to say in this regard; now he saw that others before him
had come to grips with the problem and had made a statement on it. He read on, until he came to this statement:

> The objective for Christian education is that all persons
> be aware of God through his self-disclosure, especially
> his redeeming love as revealed in Jesus Christ, and that
> they respond in faith and love — to the end that they
> may know who they are and what their human situa-
> tion means, grow as sons of God rooted in the Christian
> community, live in the spirit of God in every relation-
> ship, fulfill their common discipleship in the world, and
> abide in the Christian hope.[1]

The implications of this objective stirred Bruz; he had
no idea that so much was involved in his church school
assignment. Somehow, he had always felt the purposes of
the church school or of Christian education were in-
ferior to other aspects of education. After studying this
statement, he could see theology, psychology, and sociology
all working together in a gigantic enterprise. A quick
glance at the remainder of the introduction showed him
how this was true — here he found a section on psychology
(the characteristics of teen-agers), theology, and pedagogy
(principles and methods of teaching). A bibliography included each of these categories; moreover, he was im-
pressed to see included in the bibliography several texts he
had used in college research.

Bert Smith knew much of his Bible by heart and often
reflected upon passages as he worked with the flowers at
the Mart. Remembering his promise to find the central
message of the Bible for his report to the leadership class,
he marshaled evidence as he arranged bouquets. His assignment had seemed easy to him from the beginning.

[1] Statement of objective adopted by the members of the Cooperative Curriculum Project (Division of Christian Education, National
Council of Churches of Christ in the U.S.A., 1963).

Everyone knew John 3:16 — "For God so loved the world that he gave his only Son, that whoever believes in him should not perish but have eternal life." Bert had been able to say this verse ever since he could remember. Then another passage came to mind: "God was in Christ reconciling the world to himself" (2 Corinthians 5:19). "Need I quote more?" he thought. "It's all so simple — the heart of the gospel is right there, in those two passages."

Biblical bases for teaching

Frances Lane, unlike Bert Smith, became much involved in study as she searched the Bible for the biblical references on teaching. Since teaching had always been her specialty, she was fascinated with the term "the gift of teaching" as it appeared in the Epistles. Her first encounter with the term came in Ephesians 4:11-16. Verse eleven caught her eye: "And his gifts were that some should be apostles, some prophets, some evangelists, some pastors and teachers." What was meant by "gifts"?

Having been an English teacher before her marriage, Frances Lane was interested in construction of sentences wherever they appeared. Her usual habit of looking back for antecedents now took her to the verses which preceded this one and she was rewarded by finding reference to "gifts" as far back as verses seven and eight. She read:

> But grace was given to each of us according to the measure of Christ's gift. Therefore it is said,
> "When he ascended on high he led a host of captives,
> and he gave gifts to men."

Being inquisitive by nature, her first question came with the word "grace." "Grace," as she had always understood it, meant "unmerited favor." However, since this definition did not seem to say enough to her, she did some research, and also discussed the matter with her minister.

She found an explanation of "grace" in a Bible dictionary in the church library: "The grace of God is therefore
that quality of God's nature which is the source of men's
undeserved blessings, in particular those blessings which
have to do with their salvation from sin. . . . Christ is God's
assurance to the rebellious that he seeks only their good,
and will give of himself to the utmost to persuade them to
receive it." [2]

A teacher at heart, immediately she tried relating this to
her teaching. Todd, her most puzzling pupil, came to
mind. The prayer he had written the week before still
haunted her: "We thank thee, O Lord, for Jesus, because
he did good work trying to show us what is right, but there
are still people like me who are awful but he doesn't care
about them." [3] Todd needed to know about God's gift of
grace! To proclaim God's grace was obviously basic to
teaching, yet he had been in her class all this time and she
had failed to make clear the very heart of the gospel! Her
sense of failure was greater than ever.

She went on with her reading, skipping to verse eleven.
The sentence structure was complicated. In English class
she used to diagram sentences, and instinctively she put
this ability to work as she began diagramming the para-
graph.

Frances Lane finished the diagram, then made an outline from it. She settled back to evaluate what she saw.
The task of teaching stood out boldly with its related outcomes and attitudes. What an assignment! What a stewardship! Which teacher would feel equipped to do this,
she thought.

The concordance led her to another passage concerned
with the "gift of teaching": 1 Corinthians 12. The end of
verse three caught her attention: "And no one can say
'Jesus is Lord!' except by the Holy Spirit." Alerted by this

[2] *Harper's Bible Dictionary.* New York: Harper and Row, 1952.
Used by permission.
[3] Taken from an actual prayer written by a seventh-grade boy.

EPHESIANS 4:11-16

"And his gifts were that some should be

I. THE VARIETIES OF MINISTRY:

apostles,
some prophets,
some evangelists,
some pastors and teachers,

A. THE TASK:

for the equipment of the saints,
for the work of ministry,
for building up the body of Christ,

1. DESIRED OUTCOMES:

until we all attain
to the unity
of the faith
and of the knowledge of the Son of God,
to mature manhood,
to the measure of the stature of the fulness of Christ;

2. POSSIBLE ATTITUDES:

a) UNDESIRABLE:

so that we may no longer be children,
tossed to and fro
and carried about
with every wind of doctrine,
by the cunning of men,
by their craftiness in deceitful wiles.

b) DESIRABLE:

Rather, speaking the truth in love,
we are to grow up in every way
into him who is the head,
into Christ,
from whom the whole body,
joined and knit together
by every joint with which it is supplied,
when each part is working properly,
makes bodily growth and upbuilds itself in love."

statement she read on, noting the varieties of gifts with the role of the Spirit delineated: "All these are inspired by one and the same Spirit who apportions to each one individually as he wills" (verse 11). Introspective by nature, she immediately began a self-evaluation: "Have I been working on my own, instead of letting the Spirit lead me? Is this where I have failed as a teacher? Have I been thinking only of my own ends instead of God's?" Then she went on to the next logical question: "What *is* the function of a teacher? This is something I think we all ought to discuss at the leadership class; I'll raise the question when I give my report."

In the meantime, Norma Newcomb was searching out material that would show why Jesus was called the Master Teacher. At the top of her paper she wrote: How Did Jesus the Master Teacher Teach? Then on one side of the paper she jotted down any ideas which came to her, along with some suppositions to work on and examples to prove her points:

1. *Crowds came to hear him*

Could it be that—
he was magnetic?
he was eloquent?
he said something new?
he was a good interpreter?
he was interested in them?
he knew what his purposes were?

2. *He took time for individuals*

such as—
Simon Peter
Nicodemus
Zacchaeus
the Samaritan woman
the rich young ruler

3. *He used graphic illustrations*
     such as—
          a sower and seed
          a mustard seed
          a Pharisee and a publican
          a good Samaritan
          a pearl of great price

One by one, Norma Newcomb dealt with the possible reasons for Jesus' popularity as a teacher. No doubt there was something about Jesus that attracted people; however, she felt positive that this was more than a physical attraction. The crowds must have come for something more than eloquence, too; nor was what he said necessarily new. But he was indeed a good interpreter. How? This puzzled her for some moments. Then she remembered the reaction of the people when they recognized that he "taught as one who had authority, and not as the scribes." This meant that her last supposition must be true — that he knew what his purposes were. He had said, "For I have come down from heaven, not to do my own will, but the will of him who sent me" (John 6:38). A survey of the Gospels, especially John, gave her more evidence. A sense of mission was impelling him constantly. She thought of herself as a teacher, then of the leadership group as a whole; what pathetic reasons they had given for teaching!

In dealing with idea number two, that Jesus *took time for individuals,* Norma had written down the first five people who came to mind, though she was sure there were many more. How much time he spent with Nicodemus and Zacchaeus! He listened to their questions; he recognized their needs. He felt the worth and value of each man. As for Simon, a reader could see how much Jesus was interested in him. She recalled Jesus' warmth and concern as he said to Simon, "Simon, Simon . . . I have prayed for you" (Luke 22:31-32). This gave her a new insight into Jesus, the Teacher: "Could it be that it was for individuals — by name — that he was praying when he spent whole nights at prayer?" Then she found herself saying, "Did *I* ever pray with similar concern for each of the children in my class?"

As she studied her third observation, that Jesus *used graphic illustrations,* she noted that Jesus was thus speaking in terms that everyone could understand. The truth he was explaining might be very profound, but the illustration was so simple that any listener might be able to comprehend it and relate it to his life. She began to relate this principle to her own teaching. If Jesus were to talk to a class of adolescents like hers, what would be his choice of illustrations? How would he put his message in terms which they could understand and remember? "Here is one spot where I can surely work for improvement in *my* teaching," she thought. "I have never tried very hard to put the Bible into everyday language for them. I'm not really sure how it is done."

On the other side of her paper, Norma listed her findings. Time did not permit her to carry her research further, but she knew she had a framework for her report:

1. *He knew why he was teaching.*
2. *He felt a commission from God.*
3. *He was deeply concerned with individuals, remembering to pray for them.*
4. *He used illustrations from everyday life.*
5. *He talked in the language of the people.*

All of the members of the leadership class were present the next week when Mr. Johnson opened the session.

The teaching task of the Christian church Frances Lane and Norma Newcomb, seated side-by-side, had been in earnest discussion most of the time while the others were gathering. Both Bruz and Bert Smith seemed eager to get started.

"Well," Ralph Moody said, looking around, "did people get their homework done?"

"If you mean, did I do some research on the assignment I volunteered to do, the answer is yes," Frances Lane replied.

"It didn't seem like homework. It was fun, and rewarding, too," Norma Newcomb added.

"You know something?" Bruz looked sheepish. "I found what I was looking for — right in the teacher's book that the superintendent gave me when I began to teach! I'd never taken the time to read it before; I just assumed it would be boring."

Mr. Johnson smiled. "Perhaps this experience has told us something about homework and assignments. They *can* be fun if they are self-directed and problem-solving. Now, since you have already introduced the agenda for the evening, let us start right off with the questions raised last week and with the findings which our researchers discovered. You will remember that we were uncertain of our purposes as teachers, and of the reasons why our teaching should differ from that of other instruction. Since our own motivation for teaching is of the utmost importance, I feel that this point ought to be thought through rather thoroughly. I can see that you have found answers from your research to share with the group. Bruz, you have intrigued us all by your remarks just now; we are all interested in what you discovered. Will you start the reports?"

Bruz came right to the point. "I guess I had always thought of the church as being way behind everything else — not up-to-date like science, I mean. I supposed the church school was, well, something that was good to attend, but a little old-fashioned. Boy, did I get a jolt when I read the teacher's book! There really is such a thing as a philosophy of Christian education, written in black and white." He held up his book for all to see.

Mr. Johnson interrupted. "I see you have all brought your teaching materials with you tonight. If you will take a few minutes to look at your teachers' books right now, I think you will find out how right Bruz is." All began searching in their own books, then commenting as they found information concerning the Christian education objectives for their own age group.

Bert Smith cleared his throat. "All this is related to the two Bible verses which I was going to quote tonight. I was supposed to report on the central message of the Bible and I have two well-known Bible verses which tell this: John 3:16 and 2 Corinthians 5:19." He quoted them and added, "These say what your Christian education objectives are saying." There was an air of finality in his tone.

Instinctively, everyone turned to Mr. Johnson. "It is true, Mr. Smith," he said. "Our objectives for Christian education come out of these biblical truths, for indeed they are the incentive for our teaching. This is something which I am sure we all agree on."

"We are to proclaim God's grace," Frances Lane added. "I found that out from the Scripture passage I diagrammed."

Mr. Johnson looked at the chalkboard where Frances Lane had placed her diagrammed passage. "Yes, Mrs. Lane. Would you explain this to us?"

Frances went to the chalkboard. "I used my Bible concordance to find leads to this subject of teaching. I found that Ephesians 4:11-16 was one of the passages to study. When I first looked at it, I found it rather complicated, with so many phrases. So I did what I always used to do as an English teacher: I diagrammed the passage. In this form I could see what were the key ideas, especially from the outline I drew up along with it." She went over the passage for the group's benefit, pointing out the key ideas. "If we had any doubts on why we teach, this passage answers them. It scares me!"

No one made a comment; everyone was deep in thought.

Frances continued with her report. "My research also took me to 1 Corinthians 12." She paused while the group found this passage in their Bibles. "I found here the importance of the Holy Spirit in our teaching; I know this is something I had overlooked in my own work. In fact, as I studied this passage I came up with a question which I hope this group can help me answer: What is our function or role as teachers, with relation to the Holy Spirit?"

There was another silence. Then Mr. Johnson spoke. "This is such an awesome question, it is no wonder that we all hesitate to reply. Indeed, many times we completely overlook the place the Holy Spirit has in our teaching ministry."

The role of the Holy Spirit in our teaching

Frances Lane continued, with a puzzled frown, "I have been thinking about this ever since I found this passage. Can it be that teachers are to provide a climate or atmosphere where the Holy Spirit may work?"

"What do you mean?" asked Bruz, fingering the spring catch on his ballpoint pen.

"Let's do some group thinking about this," Mr. Johnson answered. "Can anyone suggest what would go into providing such a climate as Mrs. Lane mentioned?"

"A consecrated teacher, dedicated to Christ," Mary Bliss offered.

"And a teacher who knows his Bible," Bert Smith chimed in.

"A setting that is conducive to learning. You can't picture much being accomplished in chaos. I guess that would mean everything from arrangement of the room to the general spirit of the group," Norma Newcomb added.

"Would sound teaching methods be a part of this?" Kate Powell asked. "It seems to me that a setting would include the best that man has found in educational methods and learning theories."

"That seems sensible to me, too," Bruz commented.

"We must never set limits to the power of the Holy Spirit," Mr. Johnson remarked. "Yet I believe we are morally obligated on our part to use every legitimate means at our disposal to provide the best setting possible."

"I guess *that* gives us a real target!" Ralph Moody said

this with a touch of humor, but everyone knew he was
dead serious.

"Are we ready for the next report? I'm sure we need not
labor these last points; each of us will want to think about
them further, I know," Mr. Johnson continued. "Norma
Newcomb, what did you discover in your investigation?"

"I did my studying in a different way. I hope it is all
right," she replied.

"No two people are expected to do their research in
the same way, Mrs. Newcomb," was Mr. Johnson's answer.
"Each approaches the matter of concern from his own
background of interest and ability."

"The method *I* used was to jot down on scrap paper
ideas about Jesus as the Master Teacher. I put down
three major ideas and then listed examples that might
prove these points. The three main points were: 1. *Crowds
came to hear him;* 2. *He took time for individuals;* 3. *He
used many illustrations.*"

Norma went on to show how this procedure had helped
her come to these conclusions: 1. *Jesus knew why he was
teaching;* 2. *He felt a commission from God;* 3. *Jesus was
deeply concerned with individuals, remembering to pray
for them;* 4. *He recognized the needs of individuals;* 5.
He used illustrations from everyday life; 6. *He talked in
the language of the people.* When she had finished her
report, she added, "I can see why my own teaching is weak
— I fail in practically all of these."

"If any of us feels self-satisfied with our teaching," began Mr. Johnson, "these statements on Jesus' approach
have a lot to say, if we are ready to listen. And, if any
of us has feelings of failure, here are some ideas for im-
proving our work."

He paused, then continued: "Last week we listened to
each other as we shared reasons for our teaching in the
church school. We were dissatisfied with these reasons,
although I think we all agreed that they might have been
worthy motives for leading any other type of group. To-

night, we have turned to the Scriptures and have seen how they speak to our purposes. Our reports have all blended together in a wonderful way to show the extraordinary message we as Christians have to communicate, and something of the extent of our task. It is time for a summary, now, to see what we all have been hearing as to what makes the teaching task of the church different. Mrs. Powell, would you be our recorder again tonight?"

Kate Powell agreed and went to the chalkboard. She wrote, as the others dictated:

THE TEACHING TASK OF THE CHURCH

1. *To help persons to be aware of God through his self-disclosure, especially his redeeming love in Jesus.*
2. *To help persons to respond to Christ in faith and love.*
3. *To provide a climate where the Holy Spirit may work.*
4. *To meet the needs of individuals.*
5. *To relate people to God and his purposes for them.*
6. *To relate people to each other.*

Ralph Moody was uneasy as this was going on; finally, he spoke out. "All this makes sense and I believe it, but I can't see how 'Jesus' Trip to the Temple' fits into it, or how I get these purposes across to fifth-grade children who are not interested."

He acted as if he expected the group to disagree with him for what he had said. Instead, there were looks of sympathy.

"I know what you mean," Kate Powell said. "I keep thinking of Billy and Paul and I don't know how to 'say' all these purposes to them."

"How do we get through to children?" Ralph persisted.

"I have kindergarten-age children in my group," one of the women spoke up for the first time. "My lessons are on simple subjects like 'Being Friends'; how do they fit into these purposes?"

Mr. Johnson unfolded some charts and hung them on the wall. "Maybe these charts will help at this point. As Bruz has discovered, there have been people at work on these same problems for a long time. They have done research in all the related fields—psychology, child development, pedagogy, and others. They have asked, for instance, 'How much of the gospel is a kindergarten child, or a junior, or a junior high capable of understanding while working at his own level of development? Are children ready for certain kinds of learning at certain age levels in their life? When is a child able to grasp the meaning of such abstract concepts as faithfulness, stewardship, brotherhood?'

"In finding answers to these questions, Christian educators have had to look at the developmental tasks of each age group. Men such as Robert J. Havighurst have attempted to identify the characteristics and capabilities of a person at every stage of his physical, mental, emotional, social, and moral development. You can see by the charts I have here that there are certain tasks and skills human beings are ready to learn or perform at each level of their development. These range from learning to walk and talk and read, to learning how to play group games, getting along with persons of the opposite sex, and establishing a home of one's own. A more detailed discussion of developmental tasks may be found in two of Havighurst's books, *Developmental Tasks and Education* and *Human Development and Education,* which are on the book table at the rear of the room. Any of you may borrow these during the remaining weeks of our leadership school."

Developmental tasks and Christian education

As Mr. Johnson was talking, Ralph Moody had been following the section of the charts dealing with nine- and ten-year-olds. He appeared to be finding some of the information he sought, but seemed not yet completely satisfied.

"What *I* need, I guess," he said, "is to see how each lesson fits into the over-all picture. Take the lesson on the 'Trip to the Temple.' Most of the children had heard about it before they came to my class, and they told me so in no uncertain terms! Why do they have to have it again if they have already studied it?"

"In public schools," Frances Lane replied, "there are certain topics included year after year. Think how many times pupils hear about Abraham Lincoln, for instance."

"I still hear about him in college!" Bruz broke in.

"It's the way it is presented," Mr. Johnson added, "according to the learner's level of development. Both Bruz and the young child hear about Lincoln, but each according to his own level of understanding. So should it be with the well-known events told in the Bible. But Ralph has indicated another angle which we ought to examine at this time in our discussion — the purpose for each individual lesson and its relation to the whole. Would each of you take your teacher's book now and look at one of the lessons — any lesson? See if you can find a statement of the lesson's aim or purpose."

Norma Newcomb was the first to reply. "My course is *My Bible and I.*[4] The aim for Lesson 9 is that my pupils 'may realize the Bible offers in Jesus Christ the unfailing pattern they seek for a triumphant and happy life.' That fits into the over-all purposes which we have discussed."

Aims and objectives of lessons

Mary Bliss read hers: "This is a session in a unit entitled 'Jesus at Work.'[5] It says for the purpose: 'This session should help juniors to recognize how Jesus worked to overcome hate and prejudice among men and emphasized the worth of all persons in the sight of God, and to

[4] Course Eight, Judson Graded Series, Part 4, page 74.
[5] Year Six, Junior, Judson Graded Series, Part 4, page 94.

have an increased desire to be like Jesus in respecting all persons and in showing friendship and good will toward all.' "

"Mr. Johnson," Norma Newcomb broke in, "I know the way Ralph Moody feels. This job of teaching is bigger than I know how to handle. Like him, I have pupils who do not seem interested; yet, on the other hand, I feel the awesome responsibility of being an effective Christian teacher — such as we have stated in our purposes tonight. Frankly, I do not see how to put these two sides together."

"That's exactly my situation, too," Kate Powell nodded. "There is no doubt about our message as teachers, but how do we get it across to our Billys and Pauls?"

"— or Todd?" breathed Frances Lane.

"You have just set up an agenda for our next session!" Mr. Johnson announced. "We have spent this evening on the purpose of our teaching — or the teaching task of the Christian church. From this we have seen that we need to know those whom we teach. You say your pupils are not interested, that you cannot get things across to them. How well do you really know these pupils and their needs and interests? Surely those who work with people ought to know the people themselves."

"This is a big subject, Mr. Johnson," Norma Newcomb remarked. "Is there something we can study during this week in order to get ready for next week's discussion?" She turned to Ralph Moody, "You see, I *like* doing homework!"

"Psychology books are great for this," Bruz answered.

"What if you don't have them?" Ralph countered.

"Well," Bruz said, "my teacher's book has a section on teen-agers; probably everybody's teacher's book has a similar section on its own age group and its characteristics. After all, that's psychology!"

"Reading this material will be most helpful, in addition to what our own text includes on the subject." Mr. Johnson nodded toward the book exhibit. "There are books on our book table dealing with each of the age groups you teach. For instance, in one leadership education teaching series the titles range from *Teaching Nursery Children* through *Teaching Adults*. You may want to see them."

"I still feel it's possible to know the general characteristics of a given age group, and yet miss the importance of the person's individual differences," Frances Lane commented. "Shouldn't we be investigating this significant subject, too?"

"Most certainly," Mr. Johnson replied. "Every teacher should know the needs and interests of each person in his group. The best way to discover these is to make individual studies of each one. Why not try going through your class lists, name by name, to see what you really know about each class member? This will reveal how well you have trained your powers of observation."

Mary Bliss turned to her neighbor and whispered, "This will be hard with my three Lindas that I can't tell apart."

Bert Smith looked perturbed. "I don't see the need of this. It is what we *tell* that matters."

"After the discussion next week, Bert," Mr. Johnson answered, "I think you will see that just as the various plants at your Mart need individual treatment because of varying needs which you have discovered, so do men and women and boys and girls. Everyone who is trying to do the tremendous task of 'establishing a climate wherein the Holy Spirit may work' needs to be fully aware of this."

Mr. Johnson had opened his Bible and now he turned to it. "We have come to a good stopping-point, having returned to our original consideration of what makes our teaching assignment special. First John 1:1-5 reminds us that we proclaim 'that which we have seen and heard.' Let us close our session with the reading of it."

STUDY QUESTIONS

1. Every person who teaches brings to his teaching a background of individual talents, abilities, skills, and interests. Discuss how these factors may relate to his teaching in usefulness and enrichment.

2. What do you understand to be the central message of Christian teaching? In the light of this, what should you add to your previous discussion on "The Role of Teacher — What Is It?"

3. Make a study of your teaching materials for a philosophy of Christian education, together with its aims and objectives.

4. Secure a chart from your denominational publishing house to show how it has planned its study of content to fit the stages of human development.

5. Choose any given lesson in your teaching materials to see how its stated aims and objectives fit into the general purpose of Christian education.

6. For advanced reading on the philosophy of Christian education, read any of the following books: *The Dynamics of Christian Education*, by Iris V. Cully; *The Clue to Christian Education*, by Randolph C. Miller; *The Gift of Power*, by Lewis J. Sherrill.

3

. . . THROUGH

CONCERN FOR THOSE I TEACH

KATE POWELL LEFT THE LEADERSHIP CLASS THE SECOND night determined to discover as much as possible about her primary children. The class was large, and she admitted that she knew very little about them as individuals. Of course, Billy and Paul stood out in her mind, since the former was continually picking on the latter. Those boys so dominated the group that she realized with dismay that she hardly knew the girls, so spotless in their Sunday best, disdainfully eyeing the two roughneck boys. "If only I could conquer the problem of Billy and Paul," she thought, "then I would have time for the others. This week I shall concentrate on these two."

Kate knew a few general things about Paul. He lived in a large, well-kept house on Willow Drive, not far from her own home. She often went by his house just to see the flowers in the side garden. Kate assumed that the economic bracket of a family who lived in such a home must be high, although she had never read of their doings in the local society column. She did remember hearing Paul say, "Aw, here's my sister!" when a high school girl came into the primary classroom occasionally, calling to get Paul at the end of the session.

Concerning Paul himself, Kate noted that his outstanding characteristic was his height; he was much taller than the other second graders. Why was he larger than they? Was he older? Had he stayed back in school because he was a slow learner? Had he been a child whose birth date had prevented him from entering school in a given year? Could illness have kept him back in school? It could be, of course, that he might be a rapidly developing child, and, though large, was younger than the others! Whatever the answer, she was sure his size was a key to his maladjustment to the group. She realized she needed more information to answer her questions. Kate decided to examine the church school records.

At her first opportunity, Kate Powell went to the church school office to look over the records. She found in the file a card for Paul's family.

FAMILY NAME: Harris, Paul and Mary
Address: 29 Willow Drive
Children: Greenough, Mary Louise
                     (April 20, 1955)
            Harris, Paul Jr.
                     (December 27, 1962)
Occupation: Father: Chemist with United
            Mother: Housewife
Church Relationship:
            Mr. Harris — Roman Catholic
            Mrs. Harris — Protestant, non-
                     member
            Mary   — attends church
                         school and youth
                         fellowship
            Paul Jr.   — church school
Notations:
    Paul was in hospital when four years old for ten weeks.
    Pastor called regularly.

Kate carefully digested what she read: Paul's mother must have been married previously, and the "sister" whom Kate had seen coming for Paul was a half-sister. Paul's father was a chemist, working for the community's largest industry. Religiously, it was a divided family, but since Mrs. Harris had never joined a church, she could not be a strong Protestant. Paul had had a prolonged illness when a young child. And apparently he was young for the second grade, as shown by his December birthday.

Her picture of Paul was beginning to take shape. She resolved to call in his home; this might give her further basis for understanding him. She decided to watch for him in the neighborhood, to see who his playmates were, what his activities were, and what his play habits were like. She would invite him to her home some afternoon to play with her own boys, who, although not the same age, usually had a gang in the backyard and could easily absorb one more. In this way, she might be able to observe Paul from another angle. If she could really *know* him as well as know about him, she felt she might be able to assist him in his adjustments. She dreamed of a day when he would no longer be picked on by boys like Billy.

It was at church school the next Sunday that Kate got her first real insight into Billy. All of the boys were supposedly painting on a mural, but Billy and Paul were flourishing paint brushes at each other. Certain that Billy was the aggressor, Kate rushed to settle the dispute, isolated Billy, then stood over him while he finished the tree that was to be his contribution to the total picture. Suddenly he said, "I won't be here next week."

"Why?" she asked, panicking lest he be withdrawing from the class because of this incident.

"We're moving," he answered, in a matter-of-fact voice. "We leave tomorrow."

Kate thought rapidly. "Why haven't I heard of this before? Why would the family be moving?" Aloud she asked, "Where are you going?"

"To San Diego."

"Have you ever lived in San Diego?"

"No."

"Have you lived anywhere else besides here?"

"Oh yes, lots of places. We haven't been here very long. We just came here when Daddy went to sea."

"Has he been at sea long?"

"Six months. We don't know whether we'll see him when we get to San Diego or not."

"Do you know anybody in San Diego?"

"No. I hope we'll live near some boys my age. We didn't have any neighbors in this place and the boys at school are mean."

By now, Billy had finished painting the tree and had turned to talk to Kate as man-to-man. She thought, "Why, the boy wants someone to talk to — somebody who will listen to him, and I've never bothered to talk to him at all. And now that the door has been opened, the opportunity to help him has slipped by and I have missed it." Loath to stop this moment of confidence, she asked, "How many places have you lived in, Billy?"

"Let's see . . ." he started counting, ". . . I guess you'd say we'd lived in six places, unless you count the place where I was born. That makes seven."

And so the conversation went on. Kate now saw a lonely little boy before her, a family circle incomplete so long as the father was at sea, a child never sure of friendships, never certain of how long he would be in a community, no matter how much he liked it. Why had she been so slow in discovering this! How much this information might have helped her in understanding his aggressive behavior, which she now saw as stemming from insecurity. "I wonder how many others in this class are equally needy," she thought. "The leadership class was right. A teacher must know her pupils and their needs if what she teaches is to reach them."

Bert Smith was watering his gardenias at the Mart. He had won many prizes for his gardenias. It had taken years of study and experiment to discover what special care these plants needed, but now he knew just which spot in the Mart was best for them, where light and moisture were properly controlled, and the result was rewarding. From the gardenias he turned to the African violets. They, too, required special treatment, but he had long discovered what they needed, and he was as proud of his violets as of his gardenias. "It's all a matter of knowing what kind of soil and light these plants need," he reflected with pride. "It's when they are treated all alike, as so many housewives do, that they are a failure." Then Bert recalled Mr. Johnson's comment at the leadership class about the individuality of flowers and the individuality of people. "What was it we were supposed to do this week — to study the members of our classes, the way I do my flowers?" Bert mused over this thought, then said aloud, "I never thought about it before!"

Bert Smith began to go over the list of men and women who attended his class. One of the ladies had recently become widowed; everyone spoke of how brave she appeared. Another man's business had failed; he had put all his money into a grocery store which had not succeeded. Bert felt sorry for anyone in this position, although he had privately wondered if it had been because of poor management on the man's part. Another old man, whom everyone called "Grandpa," always attended, in spite of his advancing years. He was old and feeble; his contemporaries had already gone to their heavenly home, and Grandpa was standing looking toward them, as it were, but with feet still on the earthly shore. Next in Bert's thinking was a scientist, who attended the class occasionally; his job in atomic research took him out of town frequently. Bert had never done much to get acquainted with him; he was overawed by the man and consequently ignored him. Two maiden ladies in the class taught in the elementary school; it had never occurred to Bert until now to inquire in which of the community's ten elementary schools they taught — or what grade level. He usually was busy getting his notes arranged before class, and, since they were in the choir which sang at a service immediately after class, there was no time to make small talk with them. As Bert went on calling the roll of his class, he could not help seeing that the individuals within it made a widely diverse group. Surely they were as different as the flowers in his Mart!

Ralph Moody believed in the direct approach in all things. If he were told to become acquainted with the pupils in his class as individuals, his idea of the way to do this would be to stage a hike. Ralph had always liked hiking and mountain climbing; his children had also liked this activity and he assumed that most of his class members would, too. When he announced the hike, he was rewarded by an enthusiastic response from everyone — except Henry. The details of the hike were discussed noisily, and Ralph had the exhilarating experience of knowing that at last he had suggested something that was appealing to the group. Out of the corner of his eye he watched Henry, deciding to get him aside afterwards and find out what kept him from entering into the plans. However, when he was ready to turn to Henry, Henry was not in sight! He must have slipped out quietly, hoping no one would see him go.

On the way home from work on Monday, Ralph decided to stop at Henry's home to see what reasons he had for this attitude. As Ralph approached the house, he could hear someone playing the piano. Henry's mother answered the doorbell; Ralph had never seen her before. After he had introduced himself and described the hike, she invited him into the house to talk with Henry. Henry was at the piano. "Why, I didn't know you played the piano!" Ralph blurted with surprise. "That was good!"

Henry said nothing. His mother tried to fill the silence. "Henry's teacher says he has real talent. He practices nearly two hours every day. This, plus his paper route and stamp collection, keeps him very busy. He reads and watches television a lot, too. I really do not know how he could go on a hike with the class because of his paper route. But if he wants to work it out . . ." she said this partly to Henry, and partly to Ralph, ". . . I suppose he could go."

They both looked at Henry, who remained silent. Finally, he said, "I don't want to go on the hike."

"Why?" asked his mother. Then to Ralph she added, "Henry likes to be at home with us. He's a homebody, we say. And with boys doing all the evil things they do these days when they are out in gangs — I must say, I'm glad he prefers to be alone."

After a few words extolling hiking, Ralph left them. He was perplexed. What more could he do? One of the reasons for proposing this hike was to help Henry fit in with the group. If Henry stayed home, the gap between him and the rest of the class would become even greater.

At least, Ralph felt he knew more about Henry now. These qualities and hobbies of his were admirable, but were totally unappreciated by the rest of the class. For the first time, Ralph faced up to the problem as old as Jacob and Esau: Must all boys be alike (and like Esau), with interest in the outdoor life? It was Ralph's inclination to think that they should all respond to hiking and outdoor activities as he and his own children did; yet he had to concede that all adults did not think alike on this matter, and why should all children be alike? "It would make my teaching lots easier if they *were* alike!" he muttered.

On his way to church on Sunday morning, Bruz caught sight of George and his pals rounding the corner ahead of him in George's hot rod. They turned into George's yard and were piling out as Bruz came by. They wore old clothes and Bruz's first reaction was, "They're skipping church school again today." He was about to continue on his way when his sense of justice told him they shouldn't get away with this absenteeism. So he called to them, "Hey, fellers, you're going to be late to class!" The boys looked in his direction, then laughed. "So what?" Howie shouted. "We got more important things to do than sit around and argue!" George was saying, "This rod's got to be painted before winter gets here."

Bruz felt rebuffed and angry as he left them. At class, Sue soon led the group into a heated discussion on "What does the term 'beast' mean in the Book of Revelation?" Bruz immediately gave his opinion, then Sue took issue with him. This rallied Bruz's spirits, as the call to debate always did. In the midst of the discussion, for some reason he thought of George and his friends at work on the hot rod. Bruz himself had never been interested in cars, nor did he have the slightest mechanical ability. Privately, he even felt superior to those who did enjoy working on things mechanical. But the subject of the last leadership class now haunted him — that the teacher has a message and a commission from God to convey, and that the Bible had made it clear that no one is excluded. He had no right to let his class be dominated by a chosen few, nor should the subject matter be so academic that it had no appeal to a part of the group. A doubt now came: "But is there anything that *would* appeal to those boys? Do they really have any interest at all in God?" Bruz felt frustrated, torn in many directions, uncertain; he hoped the leadership class would help.

Frances Lane believed every word she had said concerning the importance of knowing her junior highs as persons. Yet, when the leadership class turned to this subject, she recognized that she had so much more to learn about each member. She knew, too, that the more she learned about this age group as a whole, the better equipped she would be as a teacher. It had long been her practice to read articles in popular magazines which dealt with teen-agers. She now decided to go more deeply into the subject, and so she drove over to the public library. She came home with three books on adolescent psychology. What she read fascinated her. "No wonder I find my class complex to deal with; these psychology books show how complex adolescents really are!"

Everyone was eager for the leadership class to begin its third session. On the chalkboard, Mr. Johnson had previously written the topic for discussion: "The Pupil and His Needs." He opened the discussion with this question: *"How does a teacher learn about his pupils?"* A lady from Trinity Church volunteered to write the class's suggestions on the chalkboard, and the following list resulted:

Learning about pupils

1. Examine the church records for information

Kate Powell suggested this, adding, "If only I had thought of this previously, I would not have had such a struggle in understanding the conflict between Paul and Billy. I had always supposed that Paul was backward, being so large for a second grader. Now I find it is just rapid growth and that he really is younger than the others. And I had never known that his sister is really a half-sister, or that he comes from a religiously divided home."

Mr. Johnson's comment amplified her point: "I hope you are all using the church records in order to know your students better. This is such a simple way to get information and often you will find some significant facts, such as the size of the family, a home broken by death or divorce, the birth order of the children, how often the family has moved, whether or not they have joined a church, and how frequently they attend. With younger children, you may secure their birth date and can send them birthday greetings — something which delights them and gives you a closer tie with them."

Norma Newcomb added: "Along with this, I sometimes talk to our minister about a particular child. Often he can give me some insights which I had not observed. Of course, I keep this information strictly confidential."

2. Be observant of the child in all relationships

When Kate Powell contributed this point, she said, "Most of us have a chance to see our pupils informally about the community. For instance, Paul lives not far from me. If I were observant, I could note how he gets along with his age group going to and from school and playing in the neighborhood, as well as how he gets along in church school. It has even occurred to me that I might invite him to play with my own children in our backyard.

Picking up this point, Norma Newcomb commented, "I see some of the girls in my class frequently in the drug-store. It's a good opportunity to see what they are like — trying to get attention, loud, boy-crazy. What I try to teach them at church school and what they seem to be truly interested in are poles apart. No wonder I feel a gulf between us!"

This reminded Bruz of his hot-rodders. "It was quite a while before I realized why three of my senior high boys were not coming to class. One day I saw them working on an old car when I came home from church. Since then, I see them frequently, riding up and down the streets. You're right when you say you learn a lot about people from watching them informally. I can understand now why they have not enjoyed the discussions the rest of us have been having. Their interests are not the same."

"I'm planning a hike for my class," Ralph Moody spoke up. "I think this will be a good way to get acquainted and, incidentally, to see the group in an informal way. Everyone's going, except Henry."

"This may be the place to suggest how the daily newspapers supply information on pupils," Mr. Johnson said. "School honor rolls, school activities, neighborhood news — and even court records — often divulge information about your pupils and their families."

3. Be an alert listener

Kate Powell contributed this point, too. She told the incident with Billy, how much she had learned — too late — about this boy who had been such a puzzle to her. All she had to do was listen; Billy had been waiting for someone to talk to. "I think," she added, "that we all ought to be quick to catch the significance of chance remarks and be ready to follow them up."

"That's true with the written work children do, too," Frances Lane said. "I learned something about Todd's worries when I read that prayer he wrote. There's a reading-between-the-lines that a teacher should be doing."

"People do not even need to voice anything to be saying something significant," added Mr. Johnson. "I've noted it so many times with adults. I eat in restaurants frequently and observe the same people there, meal after meal. One woman used to be there with her husband; he died several months ago and now she eats alone. You know how lonely she must be. I have overheard her speak of her church, so I suppose she is in somebody's church school class. I trust the teacher is aware of her unspoken cry!"

"The mother of one of my junior high girls tells me that her daughter will not go to any parties," Norma Newcomb commented. "She's awkward and very tall. I suspect she is left out of every activity. Isn't her refusal to attend these parties actually her way of saying 'Nobody approves of me, so I'll stay out of sight'? In my class she never speaks a word, and she has a way of slipping in and out of the room without talking to anyone."

"She's really saying volumes, Mrs. Newcomb," Mr.

Johnson agreed. "Loneliness is characteristic of old and young alike, and the symptoms, although differing according to the age, can be detected. With Billy, whom Mrs. Powell described, this came out in aggression against a boy who Billy thought had security. With junior highs like the girl you described, Mrs. Newcomb, it may take an opposite method. And Bert, your adults will offer as many clues as the children do. People whom we take for granted as well adjusted and happy may in reality be putting on a front. Solomon's prayer, 'Give unto thy servant an understanding heart, O God, for who am I to understand this, so great a people,' is apt for all teachers. How much we need this kind of wisdom!"

4. Recognize that each person is an individual

Bert Smith surprised everyone when he mentioned this point. He made it sound as if he had discovered this by himself, and Mr. Johnson gave no hint that he had planted the idea the week before. "You know," Bert said, "people are as individual as my plants are."

"Would you expand your idea?" Mr. Johnson prodded.

"Well, most housewives who try to raise gardenias do not realize how different they are from geraniums, for instance. They have to have individual treatment."

"Why?" Mr. Johnson persisted.

"Because their needs are different."

"Then you can't, as a gardener, use the same formula for each plant?"

"Of course not!"

Ralph Moody interrupted. "Then this means that I must use a different formula for each of the children in my class? How could I do it? I know Henry is unlike all the others, but isn't it my job to make him be *like them?* For instance, going on the hike — shouldn't he be made to enter into activities the majority like?"

"Henry will have to have a different formula from the others, Ralph. You have learned that he has some praiseworthy abilities. He has as much God-given right to these as the others have to theirs. Recognizing individual worth, as well as differences, is part of a Christian teacher's job. In fact, we should revise our fourth point on the chalkboard, to read: *Recognize that each person is an individual of worth.* You as teacher must take Henry for what he is, and accept him as having worth."

"Is that what is meant by the phrase I keep reading, 'accept persons as persons'?" Mary Bliss asked.

"It means accepting the Henrys and Todds and Lindas and all the rest for what they are."

"Are you saying that I should *approve* of those boys who placed tacks in each other's chairs?" the man from North Church asked with alarm.

"Acceptance does not mean approval of all their behavior," Mr. Johnson answered. "Antisocial, inconsiderate, thoughtless deeds do not deserve approval. Maybe I can illustrate this by the story of a junior high boy I know who gave trouble to everyone in school except one teacher. When asked why he behaved well for her, he replied, 'She believes in me.' Everyone needs to be 'believed in.'"

5. Make use of psychological findings on human development

It was not Bruz, but Frances Lane who mentioned this point. "Bruz reminded us at our last meeting of what information our teacher's books give on the age-level characteristics. I found this material to be most helpful. Then I went to the library and took out some of the books suggested in the resource section of my teacher's book. These, along with the articles I have read in newspapers and magazines, have certainly helped me tremendously."

"If I can work it into my schedule next semester," Bruz said, "I'd like to take a course at college on adolescent psychology. I know the course is offered. It sure would help my teaching."

6. Use home visits and community contacts

"I think we have left out one of the most important, and easiest ways to learn about our pupils," Ralph Moody said. "It doesn't take long to call at a home. Look how much I found out about Henry in a short time! Don't you agree, Mr. Johnson, that this is important?"

"Indeed I do. And I think it works two ways, for parents like to meet a child's church school teacher, also."

"I have often met the parents of my primary children at the public school PTA," Kate Powell remarked. "I've worked on committees with some of them and have come to know them well."

"I've had a similar experience when I've worked on United Fund drives," Norma Newcomb added. "In fact, it was on one of these drives, when I got teamed with the mother of the junior high girl I was telling you about, that I learned of her daughter's shyness."

"Probably I should take more time to chat with my customers at the Mart," Bert Smith ventured. "Members of my class often come in to buy flowers, but I've always kept our relationships there on a strictly business basis."

"Do you think I ought to take up hot-rodding, so I can get through to my three senior high boys?" Bruz laughed, and everyone else did too — at the tone of his voice.

"The Apostle Paul said, 'I have become all things to all men, that I might by all means save some," Bert Smith quoted glibly, with a twinkle in his eye.

The group laughed. Then Mr. Johnson said, "I guess we all see the importance of getting to know people through these outside contacts. Are we ready, now, to turn to the second problem slated for discussion tonight: *How do we discover pupils' needs?* It is one thing to know characteristics and to recognize them. It is even more important to know what the needs are of these individuals."

Discovering pupils' needs

Mr. Johnson looked around the circle, then gave some directions. "I want each of you to take a piece of paper and write down the names of your pupils. Beside each name, list as many needs as you can think of."

The room was quiet for several minutes when Bruz said, "This is hard!"

"I haven't the remotest idea of what the needs of my three Lindas are," Mary Bliss remarked. "How could I? I still can't tell them apart!" Everyone laughed.

"People *are* like plants," Bert Smith murmured. "Why, every person in my class comes from an entirely different situation from every other one! One old gentleman, perhaps, needs a discussion of heaven, while the two school teachers who attend probably have some problem from school on their mind. As for the atomic researcher in our group, I've never talked with him; I can't see how any person with his brilliance can have any need at all!"

"The very fact that he attends the class when he is in town tells you that he must come for some reason," Frances Lane answered.

When everyone had finished writing, Mr. Johnson asked, "What did you discover?"

Mary Bliss was the first to speak. "Frankly, I cannot make such a list as you asked for. As I've said before, my classes have been good, but when I attempted to make this list, I realized that I do not know the children well enough to know what their *individual* needs are. I've always thought of them as a group. How shall I begin to learn about them — by trying all of the suggestions made tonight?"

"These will certainly help you, Mrs. Bliss," Mr. Johnson replied. "But first of all, I think you can see that it is important for you to be able to distinguish each of your class members by name. No pupil, child or adult, feels he is very valuable to his teacher if the teacher often calls him by the wrong name."

"I think Henry needs an opportunity to let the other

children in the class see what he can do well," Ralph
Moody broke in. "I think they need to be put in a position where they are dependent on Henry to reach some
goal they want to achieve. I'm not sure how to do this, but
maybe we need something like a talent night where all the
classes of the church school participate, and Henry is the
representative from our class. Then, while he is being
applauded by the audience, the other fifth graders can say,
'Henry belongs to *our* group; he's *our* entry.' Maybe a
talent night isn't quite the answer, but the principle is
what I'm after."

"You are on the right track," Mr. Johnson replied. "It
may not be an all-church talent night, but some activity
within your own class that will put the group into a position of dependence upon Henry. In any event, one of
their needs is to appreciate others who are different."

"Of course, it is too late to help Billy," Kate Powell
said, thinking of her second grader who was moving away.
"I realize now that he needs security. But I think I can
see some needs that Paul has. Paul is big for his age and
this makes him self-conscious; I suspect many like me have
thought he was capable of doing more than he can, just
because he is big. I think he needs to be with other children and discover how they play. I'm not sure I am aware
of all his needs yet, but I'm going to do more study!"

"Todd has been my major concern ever since I took
the seventh grade," Frances Lane remarked, "although I
know the others in the class have needs, too. Like all
adolescents, Todd wants to feel important, and asking a
lot of questions may be a way of getting attention. He
likes one of the girls, but the girls as a whole dislike him
intensely. This rejection must hurt. He wants status and
a sense of belonging. And down deep, I am sure, he is
seeking a closer relationship with God (judging from the
prayer he wrote). But a touch of adolescent doubt is creep-
ing in. He has such a lot of needs!"

"Status, a sense of belonging, and security are basic

needs of all people, no matter what their age," Mr. Johnson added.

"I guess it's my turn," said Bruz. "When I consider my three senior high hot-rodders, I know their needs are to do something with their hands and they find satisfaction in working on an old car. The other young people in the group are just the opposite; what they want to do is to *think*, and this thinking process is sharpened by argument. Frankly, I feel the same as they do. But if what we said last week is correct — that a teacher has to convey a message and has a commission from God, with no one excluded — I see that these three boys have spiritual needs too, and my job as teacher is to do something about it. I hope this leadership class will show me what to do next about this situation. There must be other ways of getting everyone to do some deep thinking without always becoming involved in a heated argument.

"That leads us to the subject of next week's class session," Mr. Johnson replied. "I can see that everyone is ready for it. In one way or another we all have been asking how we can relate the gospel to individuals who have complex needs. How do we present a lesson that will speak to the varying types of persons in our group? Good teaching demands a variety of methods to appeal to the variety of individuals included. Next week we'll investigate some of these many techniques."

Mr. Johnson turned to Bruz, Frances Lane, and Kate Powell, and with a twinkle in his eye, said, "In addition to reading the next chapter in the textbook, will you three help me by making some special preparations for next week's session? Bruz, will you bring in a list of forty nouns — any nouns? Mrs. Lane, will you bring us an exhibit of twenty-five articles — any articles? And Mrs. Powell, will you bring in some of the coloring sheets from your primary materials?" They nodded assent — with puzzled looks. The rest of the group looked curious.

Norma Newcomb looked up from her notebook where

she was making extensive notes. "Mr. Johnson, you mentioned Solomon's prayer for understanding. I think I need that prayer to help me in my teaching role. Could you tell me where it is found?"

"I know no better way of closing our session tonight," he said, "than reading this passage together. Shall we all turn to 1 Kings 3:1-15 and read it, right now?"

STUDY QUESTIONS

1. Why is an understanding of the individual basic to Christian teaching?
2. From your own experience in groups, contrast your reactions and responses between a time when (a) your identity was well known to the leader or teacher, and when (b) you were just another face or statistic to the leader or teacher.
3. Discuss the relationship that environmental and heredity factors have upon the learner, and the subsequent task of the teacher with this learner because of this relationship.
4. Make a study of the age-level characteristics of your class; how do the members of your class compare with these general characteristics?
5. List as many means as you can think of which help a teacher to know pupils as individuals — their characteristics and needs.
6. Select two pupils in your class and compare and contrast them according to (a) physical development and appearance, (b) mental development, (c) home life, (d) social adjustment, (e) abilities and interests, (f) spiritual development, (g) needs.
7. What factors can cause a child to leave a teaching session saying, (a) "The teacher doesn't like me . . ."; (b) "That teacher makes me feel important . . ."?

4

. . . THROUGH
THE BEST MEANS
OF COMMUNICATION

WITH AN AIR OF ANTICIPATION, THE LEADERSHIP CLASS settled down for its fourth session. The assignments which Mr. Johnson had given to Bruz, Frances Lane, and Kate Powell to prepare for this session had made them all wonder what their teacher was planning to do.

However, instead of referring to the assignments, Mr. Johnson opened the session by calling attention to the objective for Christian education which the class had discussed at a previous session:

> The objective for Christian education is that all persons be aware of God through his self-disclosure, especially his redeeming love as revealed in Jesus Christ, and that they respond in faith and love — to the end that they may know who they are and what their human situation means, grow as sons of God rooted in the Christian community, live in the spirit of God in every relationship, fulfill their common discipleship in the world, and abide in the Christian hope.

"If you reduce this objective to its minimum, what do you have for purposes?" he asked.

" 'To help persons to be aware . . . and to respond,' " Frances Lane replied.

"That's right," Bruz agreed. "There are two steps: first, to be aware of God through his self-disclosure, especially his redeeming love in Jesus Christ; and second, to respond in faith and love."

Mr. Johnson went on: "Tonight our job is to investigate the *means* whereby these ends may be reached. We have already agreed, in an earlier session, that the Holy Spirit is participating in this teaching process and that our function as teachers is to be used by him in producing a climate for his work. As teachers, our consecration, good judgment, common sense, and general know-how are of maximum importance. And it is here that the teaching methods which we use enter into the process. Our over-all problem is: *By what means and by what methods are people best enabled to perceive God's self-disclosure and redeeming love in Jesus Christ?* And is it reasonable to think that all people can be reached in the same way?"

"That would be the same as saying that gardenias and geraniums respond to the same treatment!" Bert Smith spoke spontaneously.

"Teaching has always seemed to me to be like Jesus' parable of the shepherd and the lost sheep," Norma Newcomb commented. "We may find methods which reach the ninety-and-nine, but if there is one pupil who is still unreached, it is our job to try every method possible until we have helped that person, too."

"I'd have the same joy I know the shepherd in the parable must have felt when he found his lost sheep, if I could discover the approach Todd needs in order to respond to God's redeeming love!" Frances Lane confessed.

"The teaching process seems to become more complicated all the time," remarked Ralph Moody. "When I agreed to teach a class of juniors, I thought all I had to do was meet them on Sunday morning and we'd read the lesson together. That's all *my* teacher did when I was a boy."

"Did you enjoy church school as a boy?" Kate Powell queried.

"Frankly, no! I was such a poor reader that I worried all the time lest this show up!"

"Haven't we a principle involved in what Ralph has just confessed?" Frances Lane asked. "If Ralph came to class worrying that he might be called upon to read aloud, how could he possibly be open to hear God's message? His mind was so occupied with hiding his poor reading ability that he could not be alert or ready for what God was saying to him. I believe that it is important in teaching for a pupil to come with a receptive spirit, not with fear and anxiety. In Ralph's case, the teacher **The Law of Readiness** should have noticed his embarrassment and tried some other way of introducing the lesson material. Isn't that true?" She looked around the circle questioningly.

"I never thought about it before," Bruz replied, "but what you've said makes sense. I suppose those three senior high boys of mine have never learned to voice their thoughts in public, so they naturally dislike entering a class debate. But how else can we deal with the lesson?"

Ralph broke in: "Henry has developed a resentful attitude lately. He acts angry if I call on him, whereas he used to be the one I could depend on for answers. Now, when I ask questions, *no one* answers. How can you teach if no one will answer your questions?"

Mr. Johnson glanced toward Frances Lane. "Mrs. Lane, to go back to your question, there *is* a big principle at stake here. It is known as the Law of Readiness. We've just heard described what could be called foot-dragging on the part of pupils. It is the teacher's responsibility to change this situation. A climate or atmosphere needs to be established wherein the pupil feels stimulated and invited and challenged to open up, to be receptive. This is extremely important, for only when he is ready to learn can meaningful learning take place. He must be convinced that what you are going to discuss is really going to say something to him in his situation."

"Mr. Johnson," Norma Newcomb asked, "just how do we get our pupils to learn?"

Ideas of how   "The teacher tells, and they listen,"
people learn   Bert Smith answered readily.

"But when *I* tell them the lesson," Norma interrupted, "they never seem to hear. Or, at least, they do not remember."

"I believe they learn most by doing," Kate Powell said.

"Or is it by seeing?" Ralph asked.

Mr. Johnson looked around the circle, then said, "You have mentioned the traditional patterns of how people learn, and these all have their merit. However, I think we are now ready for the assignments which I have asked Frances Lane, Kate Powell, and Bruz Hendricks to prepare. This is to be an experiment. We are going to divide into three groups." (He paused long enough to divide the group into sections.) "Bruz, will you go with group A; Mrs. Lane, with group B; and Mrs. Powell, with group C?"

Mr. Johnson gave the following instructions to group A: "Bruz has prepared a list of forty words. He is going to read them slowly to you; when he has finished, each of you is to jot down as many of these words as you can recall. This is 'teaching by telling' or 'learning by listening.' "

To group B, Mr. Johnson said, "Mrs. Lane has set up an exhibit of twenty-five objects on this table. When she gives the signal, you are to come to the table and look at the objects, then return to your places to record what you saw. She will be 'showing'; see what you can learn by 'seeing.' "

To group C, he said, "Kate Powell has prepared some pictures for you to color — she has taken them from her primary activity packets. Will you color them as she instructs you? You will be 'doing.' " Kate handed out the pictures of a Bible story and placed a box of crayons on the table for everyone's use. The group went to work.

When Mr. Johnson called the entire group together

again, there were many comments as they settled in their circle. "I couldn't remember half of the objects Frances laid out on the table." "When Bruz got to some of those legal terms, I got so confused trying to remember them that I forgot some of the easier words he mentioned first." "What a pretty picture you colored, Norma! Mine is not half as nice."

Mr. Johnson turned to group A to report on their experience. "Who remembered the most words?" he asked. "Not I," Bert Smith replied. "I got only five. I found it very hard to remember them."

"It would have helped," Mary Bliss added, "if the words had had some relationship to each other. They were so unrelated, and many of them so unfamiliar, that I can remember only a few of them."

Relationships and their importance

"What do you people in group A conclude about the power of telling or the ability to learn from hearing?"

"If the words had been related to my own life, instead of to the legal profession, I think I would have remembered more." "I guess it takes more than hearing *once* to teach *me!*" "*I* wrote down some words Bruz did not read to us! I can't trust my own ears!"

Mr. Johnson turned to group B. "What conclusions did you make? Was seeing a good means for remembering?"

"It may be good for some people, but I did not recognize half of the items she had on the table; I think they must be cooking utensils!" "I gave some of them the wrong names and I remembered only ten." "If these items had all been concerned with one field — like cooking or sports — it would have been easier. I couldn't seem to relate them to any one thing."

"Group C has some lovely pictures to show us," Mr. Johnson continued. "Tell us what you have learned from this activity of coloring."

"Everyone else had the blue crayons and I never did get time to finish my picture!" "I had a lot of fun coloring, but I still don't know what the story is about." "I was reminded of my nephew. When he was little, someone asked him what he was learning about Jesus at church school. 'Learning about Jesus?' he asked. 'Why, all we do in that class is color.'"

Kate Powell sighed. "Apparently people do not always learn, even by doing," she said.

"To summarize," Mr. Johnson went on, "I think we all have discovered the inadequacy of the basic processes of hearing, seeing, and doing when they serve alone. Much more is needed in order to make them useful. I think you all saw how important *relatedness* or *relationships* are. The new words Bruz introduced and the unfamiliar objects Mrs. Lane showed were hard to remember because, first, they were not related to each other, and second, you were unable to attach them to your own previous knowledge or experience. Wise teaching offers the learner a chance to identify that which is to be learned with some previous learnings, as well as seeing its relationship to himself and his whole range of background experiences." He held up a book and pointed to it. "As Iris Cully says in her book, *The Dynamics of Christian Education,* 'The task of Christian nurture is to put [the learner's] present experience in a context that will give him something to remember.' [1] You can see how important this is."

"How do I do that?" Norma Newcomb looked worried.

How to develop awareness

"No one can tell you *how specifically* to deal with your own individual class," Mr. Johnson replied. "But it *is* possible to open doors and let you select which routes, or methods, seem most appropriate. We have already referred to the need for readiness and how the teacher must be concerned with this. And we are agreed that our first task is

[1] From *The Dynamics of Christian Education,* by Iris V. Cully. Copyright 1958, W. L. Jenkins. The Westminster Press. Used by permission.

to help persons 'be aware of God, . . . especially his redeeming love in Jesus Christ.' This leads to the next step, then: How do we produce awareness? Let's ask how *we ourselves* have become aware of God's redeeming love."

"From our relationships with people who have known it," Norma Newcomb replied quickly.

"Yes, indeed," Mr. Johnson agreed. **The role** "People are very important in the com- **of people** munication of the gospel. This means that we as teachers, through our own awareness and response, are communicating the gospel by everything we *are,* and *say,* and *do.* Practicing what we teach is imperative. Living in a state of awareness and response ourselves is our most useful and most convincing means of communicating to pupils."

"A teacher must know the Bible too," Bert Smith added. **The role**
"That's hard," Ralph Moody said, "I **of the Bible** have trouble keeping all those Bible stories and characters straight."

"The characters and events of the Bible must have meaning to the teacher before he can make the Bible meaningful to others," Mr. Johnson replied. "When persons see how these people and events are related to the whole story the Bible tells — the story of God's redemptive plan and purpose for man — then they are better able to understand how God is at work in their own lives, today."

"This involves knowing facts and acquiring information, doesn't it?" Bruz **Acquiring facts** asked. "Learning facts is boring. I hate **and information** to learn names and dates."

"For some reason, many people have an idea that learning facts and gaining information are boring, and inappropriate to Christian education," Mr. Johnson replied. "I, for one, take issue with this in two respects: first, I believe there are many ways that are not boring to acquire such knowledge; and, second, how else can a person recognize God's hand, as shown in the Bible, if he does not know the events or the situations where God was at work? For instance, to see God's providence in the Old Testament, it is necessary to know the stories of Moses and the events that took place in the wilderness, or the circumstances of the Babylonian Exile."

"Most of us recognize the importance of knowing Bible facts and events," observed Norma Newcomb. "But how can we make fact-finding and information-seeking so interesting and challenging that pupils will want to do that? I can't get my junior highs to do any homework."

Motivating assignments and research

"Pupils do have to be motivated," he answered, "and this can be done, even with sophisticated teen-agers."

"How?" Norma persisted.

"Anticipation is a wonderful tool in teaching. Or, capitalizing on their native curiosity. These often lead to self-directed assignments and home research. Oddly, more motivation sometimes will result from a chance remark like 'I'm not sure what did finally happen to the Ark of the Covenant' than from 'Be sure to read next week's lesson on what happened to the Ark' or 'I want everyone to come back to class next week with a report on what ultimately happened to the Ark of the Covenant.' Assignments which involve homework must be challenging and stimulating if teachers expect them to be done. Teenagers, especially, like to feel that they are doing work because they want to, not because they are forced into it."

"Why, that's what has happened to us — *in this class!*" Norma Newcomb exclaimed.

"You're right!" Bruz observed. "Think of the outside work *I've* done, when I thought I didn't even have the time to come to the class itself!"

Everyone laughed.

"My daughter tells about being on committees at public school," Kate Powell said. "These committees each take a different assignment on the same topic and try to work out various forms of reports. Is there any way to do something like this **Group or** in church school? Her gang gets such a **committee work** thrill out of doing this that they work harder than they would ordinarily, and they learn so much from doing their own research."

"Committee work has tremendous value as well as appeal," Mr. Johnson answered in agreement. "I was hoping someone would mention it. It has the advantage of letting pupils work cooperatively on the phase of an assignment which appeals to them most. It lets them find out things for themselves, instead of being told by someone else. They learn where to locate answers; they learn to evaluate what they find — seeing it for its worth. They have the double benefit of seeing something in print as well as determining how to report it to others. By this I mean that there are a number of ways a pupil can give a report. Some may prefer to report information by making a chart, a graph, or a poster; some write an essay or give an oral report, while others might make up a drama or diorama. Each is working in a cooperative project, within the framework of his own personal interests." He held up a book. "Chapter three of *Here's How and When,* by Armilda B. Keiser, expands this idea, if you want to read more on the subject."

"I see how this group work can be used with children," Bruz said, "but how do Bert Smith and I use it with our groups?"

"Wasn't what we did here in our leadership course at our first session — when we subdivided our group and each of us discussed given questions — an example of one way group work can be used with older groups?" Frances Lane asked. "I liked that procedure. It gave us all a chance to express ourselves, whereas many of us would have said nothing that night in the larger group."

"We had another example of it tonight," Norma New-comb added, "when we broke up into three groups and each had a different assignment. We actually accomplished three things at the same time; it was a time-saver as well as an interesting way of acquiring information."

"*I* need things spelled out clearly for me," Ralph Moody laughed in an embarrassed way. "Now tell me, how could I use this group work with 'Jesus' Trip to the Temple'?"

Mr. Johnson paused to think, then proceeded slowly: "Luke, in writing his Gospel, must have felt that this incident was significant, for he included it when the other writers did not. This naturally raises the question: Why? It is a question well worth considering. Now, let's stop to think of other questions related to 'Jesus' Trip to the Temple' which might be raised." He turned to the group for their questions.

"What *was* the Passover?" Ralph asked. "I feel very vague about it. And why was it necessary for Jesus' family to celebrate it in Jerusalem instead of in Jesus' home town of Nazareth? I've always wondered about that."

"How could a boy stay behind as long as Jesus did, without being missed?" Bruz asked.

"Would Jesus have seen the money-changers in the temple on that trip?" Frances Lane asked. "Was that the beginning of his annoyance with them?"

"Does anyone know what the temple was like? How would a boy get a chance to talk with learned men as Jesus did?" the lady from Trinity Church added.

"Enough questions have been raised to make the beginnings of a group study," Mr. Johnson interrupted. "Now, Ralph, how could use of these questions provide the basis for committee work?" He looked hopefully at Ralph. Ralph thought for a few minutes.

"Well, I have two boys who once asked if they could make maps. Maybe they could make a map of Palestine showing the route people from Nazareth would take to Jerusalem; in the meantime, another pupil might work with them and look up some information on who took the trip and why it was necessary. About the temple, there must be encyclopedias which show what the temple looked like. I have seen a floor plan somewhere; maybe two class members could look this up and draw the floor plan for us. This might include an answer to your question about the money-changers, Frances. As for the Passover, there are two children who have raised lots of questions on Jewish customs (which I could not answer). They might look up about the Passover, and maybe Henry could help them! This is what you mean by the value of committee work, isn't it, Mr. Johnson?"

"Exactly. As you proceed on something like this, you will find ideas come easily, both to you and to your class members. Just make sure that every child is included (or one idle person may waste everyone's time). Of course, you do not want the children to lose the primary purpose for this research and committee work; remember you have raised the question: Why did Luke feel this event was significant to include in his report on Jesus? When all the committee work is completed and the reports are given, make sure that everyone sees how what he has done has contributed to this answer."

Mary Bliss had been thoughtful for some minutes. Now she spoke: "This idea of committee work is certainly a good one. Do you have other helpful suggestions as to how we can get our pupils interested in the historical facts and events of the Bible?"

Mr. Johnson smiled. "You recall how little you all learned in the experiments tonight when you were unable to relate new experiences to former experiences, such as those Bruz and Mrs. Lane introduced for you to hear and see? We said then that relatedness is essential to learning. Now we should add: *Participation* is a correlative of relatedness. Cully calls this 'historical remembrance.' [2] The

---

[2] *Ibid.,* chapter 6.

teacher invites pupils to participate in Bible events along
with the Bible characters. On the surface, this seems hard

**Need for
participation
and
identification**

to do when biblical material is dealing
with people and events whose times were
so different from our own space age. But
a teacher with imagination and insight
can see how the problems of human
nature continue to be the same, and can

lead pupils to see this too. If we identify ourselves with
Bible characters, feeling their feelings within the experiences which they experience, we find we not only remember their historical situations, but we also gain insight into
God's workings in the events of their lives. At the same
time, we can better understand his workings with us."

"How do you mean? What do we do with our classes

By role playing

to produce this?" Ralph looked puzzled.
Frances Lane was leaning forward,
afire with a new thought. "Isn't this

what is meant by 'role playing'?" she asked.

"Role playing has many forms," Mr. Johnson replied.
"I suppose its simplest form is in letting yourself imagine
that you are someone else. Take Joseph in the Bible, for
instance. Imagine that you are Joseph and have just been
sold by your brothers. What would you be thinking?"

Bruz replied instantly, "Those brothers of mine always
did have a grudge against me. Wait until my father hears!"

Kate Powell was saying at the same time: "What have *I*
done? Why did they do this to me?"

Norma Newcomb added: "Where are these foreigners
taking me? I can't understand a word they are saying."

Mr. Johnson laughed. "I see you've caught the spirit of
what I mean. Did you feel more understanding for Joseph? Could you appreciate his emotions as being emotions people have today?"

"I'm not sure my children would do this," Mary Bliss
said. "They never want to say anything."

"Let them *write* their feelings, then. Perhaps as a diary

of Joseph. Some teen-agers are very self-conscious; and acting before a group, in even the simple forms, makes them giggle and frustrates the purpose of the activity. Even an activity like this needs to be adapted to your own group's characteristics and situation."

"My lessons have been on Job lately," Bert Smith remarked. "Do you suppose he would be a good character to role play?"

"If each person were to try to put himself into Job's sandals and experience what Job was experiencing, I think he would make some important discoveries about God, the way Job did."

"I hadn't thought of that," Bert replied. "Do you think adults would like this kind of thing?" He looked dubious.

"I would, and I'm an adult," Ralph Moody replied.

"So would I," Kate Powell and Norma Newcomb answered together.

"I think my high school crowd would like to do this, too," Bruz said.

"The kind of role playing I have read about included more than one participant," Frances Lane ventured. "Would you tell us more about that?"

"Do you mean we have to make up plays?" Mary Bliss continued to be unenthusiastic.

"You may have read about a form of role playing sometimes used with young people and adults, Mrs. Lane, which is a sort of an open-ended discussion. For example, suppose a problem on Christian living arises. Several members of the group may represent the various sides of the problem, with no conclusions being made."

"Could we try this right now?" Frances Lane asked. "I want to see how it is done."

"Suggest an idea to us, Bert," Mr. Johnson said.

"How about forgiving 'seventy-times-seven'?"

"All right. Let's think of a situation where forgiveness might be hard. . . ."

"How about a situation where a family in the neighborhood is noisy and messy. They won't cooperate in neighborhood clean-up drives, and their kids are always running across other people's property. That's the kind of situation we actually have now in our neighborhood." Ralph Moody offered this, and the rest nodded approval of his choice of situation.

"All right," said Mr. Johnson, "we'll role play how a person in Ralph's predicament can practice Jesus' teachings on forgiveness. Have we volunteers for the roles?"

"I'll be the noisy, uncooperative neighbor," Ralph volunteered. "I want to know what it would be like to be so slack and careless."

"I'll be the meticulous neighbor on his right," Bruz said. "I work on my premises all the time to keep them attractive."

"You'll be the one who has to practice this forgiveness Jesus mentions," Frances Lane said. "I'll be the neighbor on the left of the new man; I'm the kind of neighbor who wants to get even with him."

Mr. Johnson gave the role players some time for a huddle. "This is hard!" Bruz remarked as the role players came back to the circle. "I don't want him to borrow my lawnmower and he says he hasn't any of his own. He broke my snow shovel last winter."

For several minutes the role players represented the situation. When Mr. Johnson cut the discussion, Kate Powell said, "I didn't feel Bruz was convincing enough; I think he was too passive in his forgiveness."

Bruz turned to her. "It's a hard predicament to be in; I was not sure what to do."

"But does forgiveness mean meekly letting him take your lawnmower?" Kate persisted.

Mr. Johnson came to the rescue. "This has been a case of successful role playing, for I see it has evoked a discussion which might continue for some time. You have revealed the predicament which forgiving 'seventy-times-seven' raises, and those not in the cast have become as involved as you were as role players. Do you see how this activity can stimulate an awareness of how the gospel might speak to persons in such a situation?"

"I can," Ralph commented. "I was beginning to understand my neighbor's feelings and even getting to feel sorry for him, instead of angry."

"Role playing has that virtue," Mr. Johnson replied. "It is the putting of yourself into another's place and seeing things from his point of view."

"I'm going to use it with my young people!" Bruz declared.

"I think you are all seeing how this idea of participation and relatedness fits into teaching. Identification is so necessary a part of teaching. But let's go on to other ways of building this awareness. Do you have any suggestions?"

"Personally, I believe in audio-visuals," Norma Newcomb replied. "I think we should use lots of movies and filmstrips."   **Audio-visual teaching aids**

"These are good — if they include relatedness and opportunity for identification, and if they are introduced by and followed up by good questions and problems to solve. . . ." Mr. Johnson paused.

"We have no projector at our church," Frances Lane interposed.

"And we have no money for films!" Norma Newcomb laughed. "So you see, I'm stopped before I start!"

"What can we do if our budget is limited?" Frances Lane asked.

"There are other visual aids besides projected ones. How many of you have a chalkboard available?" Mr. Johnson   **Non-projected visual aids**
turned to the group for answers. Everyone nodded. "This is one visual aid that is indispensable. Try having something on it when the class enters the room — an interesting chart, a problem stated in a thought-provoking way, a hand-drawn map, or a stimulating list — intriguingly ar-

ranged. If you do not have chalkboard space, use a large piece of paper with this same material on it. Newsprint is good, or even brown wrapping paper will do. Use felt-tipped pens or crayons for marking. The idea is to stimulate interest through the eyegate which will lead to an awareness and, ultimately, to a *response*."

Pictures (biblical) "Our superintendent keeps reminding me that there is a cabinet of pictures in our church school office," Ralph Moody said, "but I haven't had a chance to look through them, yet."

"A church school which is equipped with pictures is lucky," Mr. Johnson replied. "Just imagine your opportunity if this set includes a picture of the temple, Ralph! Or celebration of the Passover! Here is a way of helping pupils find answers to their questions."

"If God speaks to people through different channels, I suppose some persons may be reached through pictures who would not otherwise be reached," Kate Powell observed. "This may be the way to reach a 'lost sheep' when no other means speaks to him. But we have no picture file in our church. Where can I get some religious pictures?"

"A teacher can build a library of pictures rather easily," Mr. Johnson replied, "and it is worth the effort. Denominational publishing houses carry pictures on scriptural themes. To be able to visualize biblical scenes helps young and old. Of course, you must be sure the art work is acceptable — of good quality."

Pictures (contemporary) "If you'll let me use my daughter's school teacher as an example again," Kate Powell said with a touch of apology, "I might add that she uses many pictures taken from popular magazines. She tells me that she goes through each magazine she subscribes to, just to cut out the attractive colored pictures which might have a relationship to some subject she teaches. She inspired me to do the same, and now I have quite a collection which I have mounted on bright colored paper. For instance, I have pictures of many types of churches which I use when we are studying the unit on 'The Church.' I also cut out pictures which illustrate problems of life that boys and girls have to face; I prize these particularly."

"How do you use them?" Norma Newcomb asked.

"All kinds of ways. Sometimes I simply put them around the room for atmosphere. They set the tone for the session. It's surprising how much the children look at them."

"That's all right for *children*, but you would not do it for young people, would you?" Bruz had contempt in his voice.

"I think *any pupil*, old or young, appreciates pictures," Mr. Johnson replied. "Have you noted how adults thumb through magazines to see the pictures? Mrs. Powell's words 'for atmosphere' describe this appreciation perfectly. A room that has pictures dealing with the subject you are to study leads you immediately into thinking of this subject. And, if the picture does not give obvious clues, your question is: What is this picture's connection with what we are to study? I certainly would use with young people pictures which are appropriate to their age level."

"Pictures from popular magazines would be useful when teaching subjects like the Ten Commandments, or Jesus' temptations," Frances Lane remarked.

Mr. Johnson reached to the nearby table to a pile of pictures which he had previously placed there. First he showed two copies of the same picture, one mounted and the other unmounted.

"There's no comparison in eye appeal," Bruz remarked. "The mounted one is much more attractive."

"This is a prize series which I have collected," he said as he held before them several pictures depicting the various forms of baptism. "Some are from denominational magazines, but most of them came from the popular press. You have no idea how much this set helps when we discuss the various modes of baptism."

"My class might appreciate a set like that," Bert Smith remarked.

Mr. Johnson then held up a copy of Soord's "The Lost Sheep." "A study of this picture has led us more than once into a profound study of Luke 15," he continued. "Hofmann's 'Christ in Gethsemane' can be used in a lesson on prayer or in a lesson on the last days of Jesus' life; it is most effective with young people. However, don't discount the possibility of using films and filmstrips from time to time; there are so many good ones now available that you ought to plan to make provision for their use in your Christian education budget."

"Mr. Johnson," Frances Lane spoke hesitatingly, "I have used stories with my class frequently and they seem to like them. Can stories lead to a sense of awareness of God?"

"Most certainly!" Mr. Johnson answered. "I am glad you mentioned them, because they have a tremendous power of producing identification. Jesus used this method with the parables he told. You know how a congregation identifies itself with a story when a minister uses one in his sermon. A story is useful with all ages, just as pictures and role playing and committee work are. They may be Bible stories or stories with a modern setting. The test of any of these media is whether or not they are opening doors for greater awareness of God's truth and revelation, whether or not the pupil is identifying himself with and participating in what is being done, and whether or not he is relating this to his personal needs. But most importantly, we need to ask ourselves whether or not these activities will lead him to a response such as described in our Christian education objective."

Stories, a means of identification

"How do we know if we succeed in this?" Norma Newcomb asked.

"So far, I'm sure I've failed!" Frances Lane exclaimed.

"We will never know how much has been achieved," Mr. Johnson replied. "This is what makes Christian teaching so difficult. We trust by faith that the Holy Spirit is working and that he will produce *his* ends. Yet I think it is possible to see *some* forms of response. 'By their fruits you will know them,' and in teaching we do see some fruits. In fact, it is essential that we make many check-ups to see that there is a carry-over from the state of awareness to a response. Probably creativity holds as valuable a key as any to this aspect of teaching."

"Creativity? What do you mean by that?" Ralph Moody was roused again.

"Creativity is something like the digestive process," Mr. Johnson answered. "Cully says of it: 'Creative activity results when words, ideas, or experiences

Creativity —a key to response

have made their impact on a person and he expresses them in some way of which he is capable.'[3] With some people, this may be done by discussion; with others, it may be by writing, or dramatizing, or drawing, or making something. It varies according to the individual. But in Christian education, the learner is being made aware of God's redeeming love by the many ways we have been mentioning; and the grasp of a new idea, a new insight, or understanding is a response which needs to be expressed in some appropriate manner." Mr. Johnson glanced toward the clock. "The hour is late now and there is much that can be said on this. I suggest you read some of the books on this subject which are on the book table. We will also plan to include this subject in the next two sessions of our group, as we discuss lesson planning and evaluation."

"I for one have been made aware of a lot of principles of teaching tonight," Norma Newcomb commented. "I need time to digest what I have discovered."

"If we respond to what we've heard tonight, then we

[3] *Ibid.,* p. 175.

too ought to become creative!" Bruz laughed, but there was seriousness in his tone. "These things we have discussed should have made such an impact on us that we will express them in 'some way of which we are capable.'"

"That's absolutely right," Mr. Johnson nodded. "Our periods together here should be resulting in creative teaching in our own church schools. We too need to become aware . . . and we too need to respond. This is the role of a teacher — always ready himself to learn, and always ready himself to respond." He bowed his head as he prayed aloud:

> *O fill me with Thy fullness, Lord,*
>   *Until my very heart o'erflow*
> *In kindling thought and glowing word,*
>   *Thy love to tell, Thy praise to show.*

> *O teach me, Lord, that I may teach*
>   *The precious things Thou dost impart;*
> *And wing my words, that they may reach*
>   *The hidden depths of many a heart.*

STUDY QUESTIONS

1. Look through a unit in a teacher's book and note how many methods of teaching are suggested. Discuss their role in developing an awareness of God's self-disclosure and redeeming love in Jesus Christ.
2. Select one of the methods of teaching mentioned in this chapter and make a careful study of its value, use, and limitations.
3. Discuss assignment-making and how pupils may be motivated to do homework.
4. What is meant by the term "teaching aids"? Consider ways that these implement teaching. Discuss their use with the age level you are teaching.

5

. . . THROUGH
CAREFUL LESSON PLANNING

WHEN THE MEMBERS OF THE LEADERSHIP TRAINING CLASS entered their classroom for the fifth session, they instantly spotted a large copy of Burnand's picture, "Go Ye, and Preach," arranged in a worship setting on the table beside Mr. Johnson. There was a hush of expectancy as Mr. Johnson opened the session. He asked the class members to bow their heads in prayer as he repeated the words of a familiar hymn:

> O Master, let me walk with Thee
> In lowly paths of service free;
> Tell me Thy secret; help me bear
> The strain of toil, the fret of care.
>
> Help me the slow of heart to move
> By some clear, winning word of love;
> Teach me the wayward feet to stay,
> And guide them in the homeward way.
>
> Teach me Thy patience; still with Thee
> In closer, dearer company,
> In work that keeps faith sweet and strong,
> In trust that triumphs over wrong;

In hope that sends a shining ray
Far down the future's broadening way;
In peace that only Thou canst give,
With Thee, O Master, let me live.

Amen.

All was quiet as each person entered into his own form of meditation. Mr. Johnson broke the silence: "As you have doubtless observed by now, we are using in our class sessions a variety of teaching methods which you could use in your own classes. This has been true, for instance, of our worship experiences. Now I want you to have the dual experience of making use of a resource leader in this class, and of seeing how a resource person may be used to enrich your own teaching sessions. I have asked Mrs. Louise Hope to be present tonight, to serve as our resource leader. Mrs. Hope has had many years of experience as a Christian teacher and leader in her local church and at national and state laboratory schools." He turned to her. "We certainly are glad you can be with us tonight, Mrs. Hope, and greatly appreciate your willingness to share some of your ideas and experiences."

Everyone welcomed her with a smile.

Mr. Johnson continued: "In our previous sessions together, we have discussed the purposes of teaching, the pupils we teach, plus approaches and methods which may be used in teaching. We have now reached the next stage: *How do we combine all of these factors—within the set of 'givens' which are ours?* Mrs. Hope, I am counting on you to help us see how to do this."

"Plane geometry intrigued me as a high school student," she began, "because we started with a given and tried to arrive at some ultimate conclusion, within the limitations set by it. I often think of teaching as a similar process. Each teacher is working with givens, while striving toward an ultimate goal. The givens include: (1) the *setting;* (2) the *pupils;* (3) the *curriculum;* and (4) the *variables*—factors like the weather (temperature, humidity), health (the amount of sleep pupils have had, conditions such as head colds or headaches), general mental outlook (possible friction at home or with peers before entering the classroom).

"The first three of the givens can be known, but no teacher can anticipate how the variables will enter a given session, in what proportion, or to what degree. Careful advance planning (with provision for flexibility) is the best answer. 'Plan for the best, but anticipate the worst' is the motto of one experienced teacher. She prepares two lesson plans for the day she intends to use projected audiovisuals—having an alternate plan ready in case something unexpected happens to the machine or the electricity. She learned this precaution from hard experience the day her whole lesson had been centered on a film and then the motion picture projector refused to function. Another teacher plans additional activities related to her lesson objectives, should she find extra time available toward the end of the session. Still another anticipates ways she can cut her lesson if time is at a premium."

"That's a good point for me to remember," Kate Powell whispered to the lady from Trinity Church. "I never have time to finish my lesson and usually leave everything hanging in midair. I ought to decide beforehand which activities I can cut if time is running out."

"How do you prepare your lessons, Mrs. Hope?" Norma Newcomb inquired. "Could you give us the step-by-step procedure?"

"Yes, do this," Mr. Johnson said, encouraging her.

"As you see, I am one who believes that a teacher should have a carefully-thought-out plan for each session. In fact, I am of the strong opinion that this lesson plan should be carefully recorded *in writing*."

Written lesson plans

"Why?" asked Bruz.

"If for no other reason than that it will assure us we

have prepared adequately," replied Mrs. Hope. "This is what is expected of the public school teacher, and surely we, as Christian teachers, ought to be just as careful in our preparation. Many teacher's manuals give a form to use when making out lesson plans; you may have such a form in your books." She paused, as the class members examined their teacher's texts.

"If not," she went on, "I'll show you the outline I follow in lesson planning." She went to the chalkboard and drew a simple chart:

"By the time I have filled in this form I have been forced to do some definite, clear thinking on the subject and know what I plan to do."

"A teacher has to go to class with more than an idea for the kids to bite into, if he follows that chart," Bruz commented. "That used to be my policy before I came to this leadership class." Everyone smiled at his frankness. "But supposing I had an elaborate plan like this and one of the class members posed a vital question—should I ignore it, in favor of The Plan?"

"Even in the use of lesson plans, circumstances alter cases," Mrs. Hope replied. "But the teacher who arrives at class fully prepared because of careful lesson planning, is better able to cope with the surprise questions.

"You have mentioned the given of setting, Mrs. Hope," Norma Newcomb said. "Would you expand this idea? How does this enter into lesson-planning? After all, we can't change the place where we meet!"

"No, but we can use the place allotted to us to the best advantage. In teaching and lesson-planning, I believe in carefully appraising *Lesson planning must take into consideration the setting* the setting by asking certain questions: Is the room arrangement the best? How could there be improvement? Is the furniture in good repair and of the correct size for the pupils? Is lighting adequate? What of the ventilation? (A room that is stuffy or too hot makes

A SUGGESTED FORM FOR DRAFTING
A LESSON PLAN

Date: *Topic or Subject:*

Purpose:

Lesson Outline: *Materials Needed:*

  I. Introduction

  II. Development

  III. Conclusion

    Remarks:

pupils irritable or lifeless.) Is the room clean—free of tiny paper wads which might attract alert boys, or of paper which invites the making of airplanes? Granted, there are sometimes factors over which none of us has control (like the time when a large class of juniors had to meet in the tiny choir loft because the furnace failed to heat their usual spacious room). But there are other factors pertaining to the setting which any teacher can control—distractions which can be eliminated—and teachers should feel an obligation to do so in order to pave the way for the richest possible learning experience on the part of the pupils."

"Just erasing the chalkboard before class was enough to keep my juniors from being distracted by those silly drawings and comments that usually greeted them on Sunday mornings," offered Ralph Moody.

Mrs. Hope nodded. "We said the second given in preparation concerns the individuals who make up the class. A teacher should think of each pupil individually, considering his characteristic traits and needs. Prayer for each pupil by name is vital, as well as prayer for the group as a whole. We all know that teachers are a *Lesson planning* channel through which God seeks to *must be beamed* communicate his message to those with-*to individual* in the class; therefore, the relationship *class members* between teacher and pupils must be prayerful and personal. Furthermore, I believe that in planning a session, the teacher should design the lesson for the most hard-to-reach person in the class; if that person is reached, the others will likely be reached also."

"What do you mean by the most hard-to-reach person in the class, Mrs. Hope?" Frances Lane asked.

"Do you mean the mischief-makers?" Kate Powell asked.

"The most hard-to-reach person in the class does not need to be a discipline case," Mrs. Hope explained. "In fact, this person may be someone who is so good that you have not spotted him. I am thinking right now of a high school sophomore who is brilliant but who never does anything, positive or negative, in his church school class. He comes from a deeply spiritual home and supposedly has a superior background of Christian training. Yet he seldom contributes or responds in any way in class."

"Could he be bored?" Frances Lane suggested.

"He may have reached a cynical stage and is inwardly scoffing at everything that is being said and done," Bruz commented.

"Whichever of these answers is the correct one," Mrs. Hope answered, "his teacher should be alert to these symptoms and beam the lessons to his special needs."

"Are you saying that if I design my lessons to attract the boys who are interested in hot-rods, the others in the group will also be attracted?" Bruz asked incredulously.

"It's worth trying," Mr. Johnson smiled at him. "Anyone can teach the easy members of a class; reaching the hard-to-reach takes skill, concern, prayer, perseverance."

Mrs. Hope paused, then continued. "Another concern in lesson-planning is with the given of curriculum — the subject as a whole, and the specific daily session. Most church schools provide their teachers with resource materials. These usually include a teacher's book and a copy of the pupil's text. Upon receiving these materials, I am sure you realize the importance of getting a bird's-eye view of the text — the introduction, table of contents, statement of objectives, and structure of the course, with its breakdown into units."

Planning which makes use of the curriculum

"May I ask a question?" Ralph Moody interrupted. "Just what *is* a unit?"

"Learning experiences are usually divided into units, and the term is used in general education as well as in Christian education. Perhaps you have seen a series of lessons on prayer in your teacher's book," Mrs. Hope said. "This is called a unit. For a given number of sessions you will

The meaning of unit

be concerned with the single topic of prayer. Another
time you may be concerned with a broader topic, such as
'The Life of Christ.' It may take thirteen sessions to cover
this larger unit."

"I see now," Ralph answered. "I knew the courses I
taught were divided into topics, but I didn't realize these
were called units."

"There are several possible ways of taking the next step
—that of presenting the unit, or subject," Mrs. Hope continued. "Suppose you now have a bird's-eye view of your
lesson materials; you have begun study of the specific unit.
You know what are its stated purposes and general content. You know the nature of the pupils with whom you
will be working. You know the setting where you will be.
Now your task is to bring all these factors together."

"My question at this point is, Are we supposed to do
everything that the teacher's book suggests?" Norma Newcomb was looking puzzled. "My book has some things suggested in it that *my* class could never do!"

"Of course no one is expected to follow the teacher's
book slavishly," replied Mrs. Hope. "Teacher's guides are
written for teachers in all kinds of teaching circumstances:

*Adapting
curriculum
to local
situations*
the large, well-equipped school and the
small one-room church; the school with
an expanded session and the one with
only brief class periods; the experienced
teacher and the beginning one; large
groups and small. The writer has to remember each one and provide for them all, just as we
said a teacher in planning a class session has to provide
for each member's needs. On the other hand, the teacher
must be like a housewife who cooks. Many cookbooks
give a basic recipe, followed by numerous possible adapta-
tions of it. The housewife looks upon her given — her
larder and her family's tastes — then selects the adapta-
tion which takes these into consideration. A cook or a
teacher who tries to do literally everything that he is told

to do, is headed for problems! Each suggestion in the teacher's book must be adapted to your own local situation. This is creative teaching—and this is what makes teaching stimulating!"

"That's a new idea to me," Mary Bliss remarked. "I've always adapted basic recipes in cooking, but I never thought of doing this to lesson plans. Usually when the lessons fell flat, I blamed it on the teaching materials."

"There is a very democratic way of preparing a class for a unit of study," Mrs. Hope continued. "In some books it is called a steering committee. In this case, the pupils themselves have a voice in what is to be studied, and how it is to be presented. The teacher may call together a representative committee from the class to preview a unit, say 'The Life of Christ.' **Use of a steering committee** The committee members study the topics and activities which are suggested in the teacher's text. Then they select the particular items which they feel will appeal the most to their group, set up goals to be achieved, and even suggest ways to reach these goals. Afterwards, they present their suggestions to the class as a whole, and group goals are set up. This method is especially good to use with teen-agers."

"That might solve my dilemma with my group!" Bruz exclaimed. "If I could get two of the hot-rod boys to sit down in a committee with two of my debaters, maybe we could come up with topics and goals that would get general approval."

"It might work with my junior high class," Norma Newcomb added. "I've always felt that *I* was to do all the lesson planning. In this way the young people themselves would be doing it. I like the idea."

"This approach is not feasible for everyone, any more than any other plan (or recipe) is for everyone," Mrs. Hope said. "Again, there are ways by which it may be adapted, and even younger children can set up goals when they discover the area with which their unit of study is concerned. Indeed, this is a desirable technique to use where children are accustomed to doing their own planning in public school."

"And if they are not?" Frances Lane queried.

"A teacher many times has to be the one who introduces the unit and who continues to motivate the pupils." She glanced at the form which had been placed on the board earlier. "I often think of the lesson outline as similar in structure to a speech, with an *introduction* designed to capture interest and attention, a *development* which deals with the main points of the material to be covered, and a *conclusion* which ties together what has gone before and offers opportunity for implementation."

Structure of a lesson

"The introduction is what counts, isn't it?" Bruz asked. "I hear that in speech classes."

"Yes, it is very important. This is where the interest and attention of the pupil becomes focused on what is being offered. Focusing is done by numerous ways. The room setting is one factor; pictures and articles which are displayed can set the tone for what is to be introduced. The room itself can invite a person to study and learn. Focusing can be accomplished through group study of a picture, or by a problem stated on the chalkboard, a set of true-false statements taken from material which is to be studied (or in review), or by examination of a resource article which is related to the lesson."

a) Introduction

"We've usually started off our session by reading the lesson out of our books," Ralph Moody said. "I'll surprise my class this week by trying something new!"

"The development of the lesson springs naturally from the introduction," Mrs. Hope continued. "Interest and curiosity have been stimulated by the introduction, and learning stems from problems raised and questions

b) Development

asked. I believe you discussed in your last session together some of the methods which can be used to do this. Group work is one. You found how learners may group together to do research and carry out projects. Bible study through identification and participation is another. Also role playing, stories, picture study, examination of objects, audio-visual aids."

"It seems to me that we are saying that a teacher must know how to do everything," Norma Newcomb remarked, "and I think this is impossible for most of us. For instance, I have never been able to do handicraft projects, so when it comes to constructing something like puppets or dioramas, with a class, I am helpless."

"Construction does not baffle me," Kate Powell replied, "but I am a complete failure in anything musical, and I believe primary children should have some music as part of their Christian education."

"Anything to do with pictures and art is *my* weakness," Ralph Moody added.

"Have any of you tried team teaching?" Mrs. Hope asked. No one spoke. "It helps solve this problem. Team teaching is being used successfully in public school systems and in many church schools. Essentially, it is a pooling of abilities and resources. There are many versions of team teaching. I have participated in vacation church schools where the staff worked as a team. There was a lead teacher who provided the main support for the two weeks. In addition, a person versed in music became the teacher when music was used. The person who understood art was the teacher when art was introduced. The person who was handy at crafts became the one who guided the class when this form of activity was used. Each saw his function as a part of the whole — not as a solo performance — for all of this team had worked and prayed together in planning sessions and the goals were of an overall nature."

Use of team teaching

"This sounds worth trying," Kate Powell remarked.

"It also may be a way of using some of the people of the church who have special skills but who have not felt competent to teach a class," Frances Lane added.

Mrs. Hope nodded in agreement. "And now, unless you have more questions about team teaching, we ought to talk a little about the conclusion of a lesson."

"What do you have in mind when you speak of a conclusion?" the man from North Church asked.

"I view it as that portion of the session when pupils make a response to that of which they have been made aware as the objective for Christian education states. This is that period when pupils take the words, or experiences, or ideas which they have been exposed to, and translate them into their own terms."

c) Conclusion

"Does this mean they are supposed to draw a picture of the lesson?" Ralph Moody asked. "I'd certainly need a team assistant to help me do *that!*"

Creative art

"I suggest drawing pictures only if this is the best way those in your class can express the ideas or experiences which have become meaningful to them. There are some people who express themselves best by art work. But others may find this kind of an activity a waste of time. For some, the response may take the form of creative discussion. Yet too many teachers try to conduct a discussion very early in the class session before their pupils have had a chance to digest the kind of information which would provide background for their thinking. If the teacher would plan for discussion later in the session, after information has been acquired and assimilated, then pupils would have a point of reference upon which to base their remarks."

Creative discussion

Bruz lit up. "I see now that part of *my* trouble comes from expecting senior highs to discuss when they have had very little knowledge of and experience in the Christian faith. I bet even my hot-rodders would say something in class if we first built up a foundation of information and experiences to draw upon."

"Does this mean I should offer time for discussion after I lecture?" Bert Smith asked.

Mr. Johnson answered. "It would be a step in the right direction, I am sure. You see, it would give your people a chance to take the information which you have given them and translate it into their own terms."

"What other ways can we use, besides discussion?" Norma Newcomb asked. My junior highs are so noisy when we try discussion. They all talk at the same time!"

"There are many other forms of creativity besides creative art and discussion," Mrs. Hope answered. "Creative writing is one of the most useful forms. Here the writer is free to express himself on paper, without fear that the others in the group may laugh at him. He may be writing his opinion of the topic which has been studied, an opinion which may prove completely opposite to that of the teacher! He may write a story where characters act and react as he feels people should under the given circumstances. He may write an essay in which he uses the findings which he has made. He may participate with the characters of the Bible and express himself in diary form, or by a journal, or with remarks such as the Bible character might make."

Creative writing

"Would you give us an example of one of these?" Mr. Johnson asked. "I know you brought some with you."

"Yes, I have some examples. It is not the main point in Christian education to produce polished works of literature. We are seeking response, and whether or not this response is expressed in correct grammatical terms is not of first importance. An eighth-grade boy who would never have dared express himself before his peers, wrote, after a unit on stewardship and a study of the parable of the talents:

LIFE AS I SEE IT

Life to me is borrowed or lent to me from God and I
must do as well as I can in everything and hope that I
will be able to help God and everyone.

"Writing on this same subject, an eighth-grade girl said:

Life is a something put in our care. It is our responsibility to see that we do something worthwhile with it. It
is given to us by God to take care of and to be given back
to God a hundredfold richer.

"In adolescence, sensitive students will often express
their innermost thoughts on paper. A teacher is wise who
lets them do this, and equally wise if there is no betrayal of
thoughts and authorship to the rest of the group. It was
in such a written relationship that one junior high teacher
discovered that a pupil claimed to be an atheist; the boy
had never dared express this aloud. This discovery enabled the teacher to help the boy reconstruct his thinking.

"I'll try this with my own junior highs," Norma Newcomb exclaimed. "Maybe they will *write,* even if they will
never talk sensibly in class!"

"My experience would say this could happen," Mrs.
Hope replied. She took from her folder another paper.
"This was written by a sixth-grade boy who was studying
about Joshua; he is writing a diary as if he were Joshua; I
think he is learning about God at the same time.

JOSHUA'S DIARY

Dear Diary:
    Tonight I'm disgusted with the whole congregation
and everything to do with them. Here they sit in camp,
crying for nothing. Why, they haven't tried to take the
land that God has promised us. They don't have any
faith left in Moses, or even in God, for that matter.

Dear Diary:

We have just had another terrible blow. Aaron has died. At least we still have a priest. We will see if Eleazar can bear his great duties as well as Aaron.

Dear Diary:

I have just had laid upon me the greatest honor of my life. I have been chosen to lead the people of Israel.

Dear Diary:

I had faith in our Lord and he did not fail me. Our first great barrier is crossed. God allowed us to pass across the Jordan River without accident. I sincerely believe if we do not offend him, he will be with us and will help us conquer our promised land.

"Say, this shows me something else I could have done with my class," Ralph exclaimed. "We could have written a journal on 'My Trip to the Temple.'" Mr. Johnson nodded, with a pleased smile.

"Narrative writing is a wonderfully objective way to get pupils to discuss a problem," Mrs. Hope continued. "Sometimes I give them a setting, characters, and a problem — then let them work with these givens. Sometimes I give them the opening sentence of a story, and ask them to finish the story — putting into action whatever teaching we have been discussing. Or, again, I let them have free rein in choice of plot, setting, and characters."

"Would you give us an example?" Norma Newcomb asked.

Mrs. Hope paused to think, then answered, "Here is an example: 'When Tom went into the store, not a person was in sight. He. . . .' This starts a class easily on an application of the Ten Commandments."

"I like this idea of having children write stories which incorporate the truths and ideas they have been learning," Frances Lane said. "Maybe Todd, my seventh-grade problem child, would project some of his real feelings into the characters he uses!"

"Of course, drama is another such form of creativity; it too translates ideas into action. This is especially effective in younger classes."

Creative drama   "I have children who love to make up plays," Kate Powell remarked.

"Mrs. Hope," Mr. Johnson said, "by many practical ways you have helped us see how to plan lessons. I know there is much more you could say on this subject, but our time is up. The book list which you prepared for us recommends books that expand the discussion on these subjects." He distributed the lists. "I note *Here's How and When,* by Armilda Keiser; *Creative Activities,* by Rebecca Rice; *The Teacher and Young Teens* and *Wide As the World,* by Louise Griffiths; *Role-Playing,* by Alan Klein; and *Tools for Teaching,* by George Adkins. Each of you will note that there are books suggested for your age group, too." He turned to Mrs. Hope, "We do appreciate your contribution and thank you for coming to our session."

There was a chorus of "thank yous."

"You've opened a lot of doors for me," Frances Lane remarked. "I can see so many ways to improve my teaching."

"I can hardly wait to try out all these new ideas," Norma Newcomb added enthusiastically. She placed the book list in her notebook.

"It was very interesting," Bert Smith said politely and with sincerity.

"The value of all our five sessions together shows up in our active response to what has been heard," Mr. Johnson summarized. "We have mentioned evaluation frequently as a necessary part of the teaching process. Next week we will investigate this subject and see how it works."

"Does this mean you're going to give us a test?" Ralph Moody asked, both humorously and with concern.

"Come next week, Ralph, and see!" Bruz countered, as he started toward the door.

STUDY QUESTIONS

1. Make a thorough study of the givens within your teaching situation. Are there factors which could be changed to improve the situation? Which factors must be accepted, and how can the problems they present be surmounted?

2. Using the curriculum that your church school provides, study a unit for its purposes, plan of presentation, and suggested techniques of teaching.

3. Make a written lesson plan for a session using the givens of your teaching situation.

4. How can the conclusion of a lesson avoid preachiness? In what ways do teaching and preaching differ in evoking response?

5. Discuss the role of creativity in teaching.

6. How can worship be an integral part of the teaching session? When should worship be used as an introduction? Within the body of a session? At the end?

6

. . . THROUGH
HONEST EVALUATION

RALPH MOODY'S FIRST REMARK, AS HE ENTERED THE CLASS-room for the final session of the leadership training school, was: "Is everyone ready for a test?"

Kate Powell turned to Mr. Johnson. "Are you really going to give us a test?" she asked. "I get scared even if the word is mentioned!"

"Me, too," Ralph agreed, before Mr. Johnson could answer. "When a school teacher used to announce a surprise quiz, I'd forget everything I knew about the subject."

"But often it is the only way to discover how much pupils have learned," Frances Lane defended. "I found tests essential in teaching English. Maybe we should do more testing in Christian education. . . ." she looked inquiringly at Mr. Johnson. "What do you think?"

Tests as a means of evaluation

Mr. Johnson had been listening, amused. "By the end of tonight's session you may have the answer," he said. "As you already know, we are to discuss evaluation in teaching. It is a many-sided subject. But since Ralph has brought up the subject of tests and Mrs. Lane has recommended their use, let's turn to testing first. Tests are certainly a form of evaluation and represent a common practice for discovering how much has been learned. There are many types of tests." He turned to Kate Powell. "You

Kinds of tests asked if we were to have a test. How would we go about testing ourselves in this class? What kind of a test would be appropriate to examine our own leadership class on what it has learned?" He turned to the group as a whole. "What do you suggest?"

Bruz opened the discussion. "During

1) Objective my years at school, I've taken hundreds of objective tests — true-false, multiple choice, fill in the blanks. They are used when the teacher wants to find out if certain facts have been learned. But I do not see how we could use this kind of test in this class, since we have not been studying facts. . . ." His voice trailed off as he pondered.

"When I was in school," Norma New-

2) Listing comb suggested, "we had tests which asked us to make lists, like 'name four ways to. . . .' I think we could use that type of question as a means to test ourselves."

"Essay tests with thought questions

3) Essay are valuable measurements when testing a situation like ours," Frances Lane added with confidence.

"You're right," Mr. Johnson continued. "You have mentioned some *kinds* of tests. Now let us consider the questions to be used. Composing questions appears to be easy, but actually, it is a complicated art. The question

The art of must be worded in such a clear-cut fash-
questioning ion that the one questioned understands its intent, and is able to respond; on the other hand, it must bring forth the kind of response that may be judged by the questioner as showing knowledge of the subject, or growth and understanding."

"I know what you mean when you say composing questions is hard," Ralph Moody exclaimed. "This is what happens in my class: I ask a simple question and a pupil replies 'yes' (or 'no'). Then there is silence. So I ask 'Why? Why did you say "yes"?' There's another silence; apparently the one who answered doesn't know why he gave that answer. By the time I've dug the reason out, the point of the discussion has gone flat."

"I've had that happen, too," Mary Bliss commented.

"The way a question is worded makes the difference in what kind of a response results," Mr. Johnson replied. "There are many poorly-worded questions that get asked in classes, both in tests and in oral discussion." He reached for a pile of mimeographed papers on the table beside him. "On this paper," he said, "are fifteen actual questions which teachers asked in classes. Please study these questions and rate them for what you think they are worth."

The room was quiet as each studied the list.

" 'Did Jesus enjoy being at the Temple when he was twelve?' " Ralph quoted aloud from the paper. "I can picture my juniors with a question like that. I'd have to push and prod to get them to give a reason for their answer of 'yes.' "

"I consider that question weak," Bruz said. "It is putting an answer into their mouths; you can feel the teacher will pounce upon any pupil who answers 'no!' "

" 'How about the publicans? Were they friends of Jesus?' " Bert Smith read from the list. "That sounds all right to me."

"Couldn't it be stated more concisely, reading: 'Were the publicans friends of Jesus?' " Mary Bliss asked.

"That leads to a 'yes' or 'no' answer," Ralph laughed. "I'd have to ask the usual 'why?' if I put that question to my class."

"What was the relationship between Jesus and the publicans?" Frances Lane reworded the question.

"That's good," Mr. Johnson agreed. "That opens the door for use of information which has been studied, as well as for some creative thinking on the part of the pupils."

"As I look through this list," Frances Lane added, "it seems as if the best questions are the ones which begin with 'What,' 'Who,' 'When,' 'Where,' 'Why,' or 'How.' These words demand some information or reasoning. Furthermore, the word 'why,' as Ralph referred to it earlier, will not need to be tacked on in an offensive way."

"Generally speaking, questions which call for an answer of 'yes' or 'no' are weakly stated," Mr. Johnson summed up. "These usually do need to be followed up by 'why?' and this weakens the questioning. It is much more thought-provoking to ask questions which begin with 'why?' unless you want to review facts; in this case, you would begin with 'who,' 'what,' 'where,' 'when,' or 'how.' A teacher needs to be highly critical when considering the questions he wants to ask."

"To go back to the list of questions on this paper," Kate Powell said, "there is one I do not like, and I'm not sure why." She read, "Did Mike break one of the Ten Commandments? If so, which one?"

Bruz replied. "Isn't it implied in the first question that the questioner considers that Mike did break one of the Ten Commandments? The answer is expected to be 'yes.' Since this is obvious, could these two questions be incorporated into one, and read, 'Which of the Ten Commandments did Mike break?' "

Mr. Johnson nodded in agreement. "You see that the wording of questions is often dull, obvious, and deadening to creative thought. To go back to the subject of testing our own class on what has been learned these past weeks, let's see if we can word some appropriate questions to discover what has been learned."

" 'How does a teacher learn the needs of pupils?' " Bert Smith surprised everyone with this contribution.

"That's a good question," Mr. Johnson replied. "Anyone who had been made aware of this subject here in class could respond with ideas which would show what had been learned."

"What are the steps that are necessary when planning a lesson?" Norma Newcomb suggested.

"That's a reasonable question to answer," Mary Bliss replied. "We covered this in study and discussion."

"What is the role of the Holy Spirit in the teaching process?" Frances Lane added.

"That invites discussion," Bruz answered.

Ralph Moody turned to Kate Powell. "A test *like this* wouldn't scare me — I think I know the answers!"

"*Anyone would* who has listened carefully in class and has really gotten involved in class assignments and discussion." She paused, then said, "Mr. Johnson, I am thinking of a session I had several weeks ago with my class. We had been study- **Putting what** ing 'Love Thy Neighbor' and Billy had **is learned** been so quick to catch the idea in class. **into practice** After church, when I was on my way home, I saw Billy teasing Paul until Paul began punching Billy. Billy knew in his mind about loving his neighbor, but he did not practice it. Wasn't this a test of what he had learned, and didn't he flunk? Is *practicing* what has been learned a part of testing and evaluation?"

Mr. Johnson smiled. "I am glad you mentioned this," he said, "for it is the practice of what has been studied which proves the depth of learning." His smile broadened as he continued. "Let's ask ourselves a similar question: In what ways have you put into practice ideas or information which have been discussed in this class?"

There was an awkward silence which Bruz broke: "I plan to ask two of my senior high hot-rodders to meet with two of our regular class members to discuss future topics for our class, but I've had some extra papers to write for one of my college courses and so I haven't gotten around to it yet."

Kate Powell added, "I invited Paul to play in the yard with my boys, but so far he has not come. I don't know why. Perhaps if I name a specific time, he'll come?" Her voice trailed off in a question.

Bert Smith looked pleased with himself. "After the lecture last Sunday, I called for questions and comments. At least three people spoke up."

Ralph Moody beamed as he said: "Last Sunday I tried a new introduction to the lesson, instead of reading it from the book. Our lesson was on 'Jesus Calls His Disciples.' I'd taken a picture on that topic from the church school file and held it up before the class (just as Mrs. Hope suggested, for focusing their attention). Believe it or not, they really did focus their attention on it! It showed Jesus at the seaside and we got into a discussion about fishing in those days. That led to a discussion on what it meant for those men to give up fishing and go with Jesus. Even Henry entered into the discussion, without my prodding."

"I wish as much progress had been made with Todd," Frances Lane sighed. "But I haven't given up yet. It takes more than a few weeks, I keep telling myself, to reach a boy as mixed up as he is."

"Jesus must have been discouraged with Peter many times during the three years he was instructing him!" Mr. Johnson commented.

"I gave my class a chance to write a story using ideas we had had in our lesson, and they did very well. I had no idea some of them could express themselves so clearly," Norma Newcomb contributed.

Mr. Johnson looked around the circle. "You've done well with the test," he nodded approvingly.

"Could I ask a question now?" Norma Newcomb asked. "I wonder how many of us sensed the variety in presentation which we've been having here in our own class. Actually, we have been doing here in our classroom just what we were discovering must be done in the classrooms where we teach." Norma held up the notebook in which she had been faithfully recording notes since the first session. "I've been going back over my notes, to see how many methods and approaches have been used; I'm amazed! Could we take time to make a list of them, Mr. Johnson?"

Evaluation by review

Mr. Johnson looked pleased as he said, "A review like this is yet another form of evaluation. Would someone write these on the chalkboard as we name them?" The woman from Trinity Church volunteered.

Norma Newcomb contributed the first item. She said, "The *small group discussions* which we had the first night."

"We made a list that night which we put on the chalkboard," Frances Lane remarked. "I have a copy of that in my notes. *Listing* is an approach worth mentioning."

"Should we count the *research* that went on at home?" Bruz asked. "Remember how I looked up the philosophy of teaching and found the objective for Christian education in my teacher's book?"

Everyone laughed appreciatively. Kate Powell added, "And there was the analysis of the Bible passages which Frances Lane brought in, concerned with the biblical reasons for teaching. I had never thought of *using skills which I already had* (like Frances' skill in diagramming sentences) to help me in teaching."

Ralph Moody glanced at Bert Smith. "That was true with Bert, too. He found that his knowledge of the differences in plants helped him to see the differences within the membership of his adult class."

Bert Smith nodded back to Ralph, as he replied, "Well, how about your own method of research when you used your hobby of hiking to find out more about the boys in your class?"

"Isn't problem-solving considered a way of teaching?" Frances Lane inquired. "We have done a lot of that. Remember how we worked on the problem of 'How does a teacher learn about his pupils?'"

"Put *problem-solving* on the list," Mr. Johnson directed. "It certainly is one of the best ways of motivating interest."

"We used *experimentation*," Norma Newcomb continued. "We did experiments in seeing, hearing, and doing."

"That was good," Bert Smith commented. "I had no idea I had such a poor memory." Suddenly he looked troubled. "Do you suppose my adults have memories as bad as mine — after all the work I put into those lectures?"

Bruz leaned forward, and spoke impressively, "I read recently that a study has been made of the listening habits of college freshmen. It was discovered that they retain about 50 per cent of a ten-minute lecture on immediate recall and even lose half of that within a forty-eight-hour period."[1]

"We talked about *participation* as a part of the learning process," Norma added, looking up from her notes. "I think we ourselves participated in our own learning process. Remember how we actually did role playing, for instance?"

The woman from Trinity Church wiped chalkdust from her suit. "Think of how many times we made use of this chalkboard! Don't we call this a use of *visual aids?*"

"Yes," Kate Powell added, "Mr. Johnson discussed all kinds of *teaching aids* and had *samples* of them here which he used."

"He showed us the value of *reference books*," Norma continued, as she looked up from her notes. "He had some with him, and quoted from them."

"I thought it was helpful to bring in a special *resource*

[1] Based on a report by Professor H. E. Jones, of Columbia University, "Experimental Studies of College Training" (the effect of examination on the permanence of learning), *Archives of Psychology,* Columbia University (1923), Number 68.

leader. Mrs. Hope gave us many good ideas," Mary Bliss said quietly.

"Isn't the *use of examples* a means of teaching?" Ralph Moody asked. "Mrs. Hope demonstrated what can be done in creative teaching when she read us samples like the 'Diary of Joshua.' "

"Frankly," Bruz said, "I've learned a lot about discussion by the actual *discussions* we have had here. It's been a demonstration to me of what a discussion can be like."

"Right!" said the man from North Church. "Say, we ought to add *demonstration* to our list, too."

Bert Smith cleared his throat. "I had thought that the worship which accompanies teaching had to be a formal service. We always open our adult class with two hymns, a prayer, and a responsive reading. Here in this class, Mr. Johnson has not had that kind of worship. . . ."

Ralph Moody interrupted, "I *like* the kind of worship we have had here. It has been a meaningful part of our sessions."

"And I've appreciated having our moments of worship at an unscheduled time," Norma Newcomb added. "They came when I was mentally and spiritually prepared for them, not just because the clock said it was a certain time."

Mr. Johnson spoke up. "I have listened to this evaluation of our class with much interest," he said, "for I think you have been examining what has been happening here and seeing how this relates to your own situations."

Bruz had been looking thoughtful for some time. Finally he spoke. "I understand how to judge the degree of learning which has taken place by giving tests, or by oral questioning, or even by review. My **The teacher's self-evaluation** problem is concerned with a *testing of myself* as a teacher. I had been blaming my senior high boys for skipping class, when maybe it wasn't their fault!"

Mr. Johnson looked at him sympathetically. "Bruz, you

are being very honest — the first requirement of a teacher. It is much more comfortable to the ego to have some scapegoat to place blame upon, but an honest teacher must always look first to himself when there has been failure. Before saying, 'It's the children's fault; they do not want to learn,' or, 'The room I teach in is too crowded,' or offering some other alibi, the teacher needs to heed the biblical advice to 'first take the log out of [his] own eye, and then [he] will see clearly to take the speck out of [his] brother's eye.' "

Evaluation of class sessions

"Mr. Johnson," Bruz continued earnestly, "I keep thinking that if I had been more observant, I might have noticed what the weakness was in my teaching. Tell me, how might I have discovered this earlier?"

"Get a tape recorder!" Ralph Moody joked. "The playback would show you who did the talking in class."

1) By tape recorder

"That's a good idea," Frances Lane said seriously. "It would provide an accurate check on all that went on in class."

"Evaluating the degree of involvement in a discussion and in class participation is important. You will find many books which describe this process, Bruz, if you want to learn more," Mr. Johnson said. "Some specialists in this field recommend the use of an observer as a co-teacher who week-by-week sits quietly, unobtrusively, in a room where discussion is being conducted, recording the degree and nature of participation of all present. He may do this by making a diagram which, at the end of the session, will show exactly how many times each member has participated. Another way to do this is by evaluating the tone of a discussion — checking for sarcasm, belittling, overtalking, splitting hairs, appreciations, suggestions. The observer may also be watching to see what progress is made within the content of the discus-

2) By an observer

sion: have new ideas been projected? were they worthwhile? what became of these ideas? how often did the discussion get off the track?"

"This would help," Bruz said, "except that our church school is short of workers and I'm not sure a competent observer could be found. But I think I see now one way I, myself, might be able to do some evaluating. I could go over the roll **3) By watching** after class each week and ask myself as **pupils'** I came to each name, 'To what degree **participation** did this person participate today?' If I had done this earlier, I might have noted that some were participating little or not at all and have taken steps to see that they did get involved, instead of letting them drop out of the class."

"Indeed, that is a method any teacher can and should employ," Mr. Johnson replied.

"Does this mean that a naturally quiet person must *say* something in class?" Kate Powell asked. "Should we consider the session a failure if such a person has not spoken?"

Mary Bliss answered. "A person can learn, without speaking out, I think. I have not talked here in class very much, but I have been learning. Talking a lot in class is not necessarily an indication of learning and involvement." Some of the other members of the class nodded in agreement.

"There are many other signs of learning, to be sure," Mr. Johnson commented. "For instance, a teacher should be watching to see what is happening in pupils' relationships with one another. **4) By observing** Is there a sign of growth in understand- **pupils' growth** ing and appreciation of each other? What **in Christian** signs of Christian qualities appear? What **qualities** evidence of response to the Christian message do you detect? Going over the roll, with these in mind, is a healthy way to evaluate."

Mr. Johnson reached to another pile of mimeographed

papers on his supply table. "I think we had best consider
this through the case study which I have here," he said.
"Sessions can seldom be judged as all plus or all minus.

Objective
evaluation
by the case
study method

The variables which Mrs. Hope mentioned govern this, and unexpected turns
may take place within the framework
of the planned session. A teacher therefore needs to weigh each factor as it
happens, and after the class session is

over, evaluate it as a part of the session as a whole."

He distributed the papers. "On this paper is a report
of a class session as related by the teacher. Let's evaluate
it for its plus and minus factors, noting how they enter
in." He read aloud, as the others followed silently:

As my sixth grade class was gathering, one Sunday, the
boys and girls went to work on a chalkboard mural
which had been planned the week before. Claudia, the
smallest of the girls, was chattering with the rest, when
suddenly she said, "I'm going to be a minister when I
grow up." There was a gasp from one of the girls, a
horrified murmur from the rest, and Doug, spokesman
for the boys, said, "Women don't become ministers."
"Oh yes, they do," Claudia retorted. Doug snorted and
his buddies echoed him.

At this point, two newcomers entered the room and I
took some time to greet them. When I turned back to
the group at the chalkboard, I discovered them giggling.
Hearts drawn with the names of Doug and Claudia
linked together had been added to the mural; amid
cheers and jeers, Doug was furiously erasing these.

The class wanted to write a class prayer to be used
weekly. A list of things which should be included was
being made. This led to discussion of situations which
arise at school and at home where lies have been told.
Madge felt the prayer should include the need for forgiveness. Helen said, "We ought to remember that we

are not perfect — what's the word to use — *humble?*" The question arose, "Should we put our words of thanks and praise at the opening of the prayer, or should we begin it by stating our present situation, where we feel the need of forgiveness? Joe, a newcomer to the church who was just beginning to get a glimmer of the meaning of the Christian message, said, "Put our condition as we are, right now, at the beginning of the prayer — then praise God." Claudia spoke with assurance, "I have a pattern when I pray and it says to always begin with praise and thanks to God."

Because the making of the prayer was taking more time than seemed proportionate, and because several class members were showing signs of fatigue, I suggested that a committee be set up to complete the prayer, doing this at the presession next time.

We changed gears and proceeded with a review of the Exodus which had been our topic in weeks past. Mention was made of the city of "Raamses" built by the Hebrew slaves. "Oh," Claudia exclaimed, "was that Rameses II?" Doug and his gang quickly exchanged glances and grins; even Madge joined them in a knowing look. Helen and Claudia remembered nearly every item mentioned in the review.

Jake arrived late. An attempt was made to orient him to what the class was doing, but I felt a lag with the others, while this was going on, and that Jake never did get caught into the discussion.

As we were reviewing the burning bush episode, Claudia suddenly spoke up. "I know this isn't on the subject," she said, "but I found out who the oldest man in the Bible was — he was Methuselah. Usually men lived about four hundred years in his day, but he lived (her eyes opened wide as she spoke dramatically) *nine hundred and sixty-nine years!*" Doug scoffed. "How could anyone live that long?" It was some time before the pupils would leave this subject so we could continue discussion of the burning bush. This changed the proposed timing which I had set for the lesson, and when the church school was dismissed, soon after, my class had accomplished nothing!

"It sounds like a battle between the sexes!" Ralph Moody exclaimed.

"That teacher has problems of inter-pupil relationships!" Frances Lane commented.

"Certainly there needs to be greater appreciation of Claudia by the boys," Kate Powell added. "She sounds like a bright little girl."

"The teacher is caught in the preadolescent problem of sixth-grade boys who frequently 'hate girls,' and Claudia represents a tangible target toward which they can hurl their feelings," Mr. Johnson said. "This teacher must evaluate each session with knowledge of child psychology in mind, asking just how much of this feuding is normal, and just how much can be accomplished with this age group in promoting Christian understanding and appreciation of peers."

Knowledge of age group characteristics and psychology as measuring rods

"Did you notice the plus signs?" Frances Lane asked. "Apparently Claudia has become interested in Bible study and has been doing some independent research. Also, she is relating knowledge she has acquired in public school to what she is studying in the church school."

Recognizing plus and minus factors in sessions

"I thought the suggestions on forgiveness and humility were especially good. The teacher ought to feel that here is a sign of positive growth," Norma Newcomb added.

"My concern is for Joe, the newcomer," Ralph Moody said. "How can the teacher save Joe's self-respect and, at the same time, show appreciation for Claudia's comments when she tells what she thinks the structure of a prayer has to be?"

"Joe's contribution is surely a plus," Bruz added. "I bet it's the first time he has ever said this much in class."

"The teacher reports that she had accomplished nothing by the time the class was dismissed, and I know how she felt," Frances Lane said. "But I've come to wonder. . . . Should every session leave us with a sense of accomplishment, or should we see our teaching as a part of a whole, and even if today we do not seem to make much progress, hope to see something being accomplished over a longer period of time?" She said this both as a statement and as a question.

Mr. Johnson responded to her remark. "I think we have to see our teaching both with nearsighted and farsighted glasses, so to speak. We do have to look at the achievements of the present, but we must also see them in terms of a longer view. It will take the teacher in this case study a long time to bring together the strong personalities in her class, and it may take a variety of experiences to accomplish this. Undoubtedly she will leave at the end of some sessions with a strong sense of failure. Most assuredly she should watch for positive signs of growth, small as they may be. Spiritual growth is slow in children, and there are times of retrogression which must be reckoned with. Before giving up in despair, a teacher must take this into consideration."

Seeing sessions from the long view

"Shouldn't the teacher have continued the activity of making a prayer until it was completed?" Bert Smith asked. "I've always believed a project started should be seen through until completion."

"Generally speaking, I would agree," Mr. Johnson answered, "but experience tells us that fatigue points come, and little learning is accomplished after the pupils' interest lags. It seems to me that the teacher was wise to let a committee continue from that point, since they were planning to go right to work on it when they arrived the next week."

"I'd like to see a demonstration of a class in action," Ralph Moody said.

"My cousin recently went to a laboratory school for church school teachers," Mary Bliss remarked. "She was so enthusiastic."

"What do you know about laboratory schools, Mr. Johnson?" Kate Powell asked.

Laboratory schools for teachers

"It has been my privilege to work in a number of them," he replied. "These schools, which are sometimes called 'demonstration' or 'observation-practice' schools, offer many advantages. Essentially, they provide opportunity for apprentice teachers to observe experienced teachers handle a class in a teaching situation.

"The length of such training schools differs — some are two weeks and some one week. The pattern also varies according to area needs and circumstances. The trainees learn how to observe and analyze teaching, and usually, as they get more experience, they do some of the teaching themselves under the guidance of the skilled lead teacher."

"I'd be scared to death to do it in the presence of observers!" Norma Newcomb commented to Mary Bliss, who was sitting beside her.

"Do you mean that the other observers criticize what the apprentice teacher has just done?" Mary Bliss asked.

"In a kindly way," he replied.

"It's like the practice teaching we had to do when preparing for public school teaching," Frances Lane commented. "I'll never forget the day when my professor from the University came to see me in the ninth-grade English class I had been teaching! I was nervous and made all kinds of mistakes. But later, when he analyzed the session with me, I could see that his suggestions were very helpful. I think a teacher has to be big enough to accept constructive criticism."

"Usually the pattern of such a school is twofold," Mr. Johnson continued. "First, the skilled teacher has a teaching session with the children while the trainees observe, and then, after the children have been dismissed, the leader holds an evaluation period with the learning teachers, where an analysis is made of what has transpired. The teacher explains what was being attempted, and how he had aimed to meet these purposes."

"Isn't there too much control in such a situation?" Bruz asked. "Does anything ever go wrong, the way it does in our classes?"

"The fluorescent light in my classroom started to flicker last Sunday," Ralph Moody commented to Bruz, "and as it flickered, my juniors got hilarious. There wasn't a thing I could do — with them, or with the light."

Mr. Johnson said in reply, "It is my own feeling that a laboratory school should have some of these realistic factors, or it *will* be controlled, as you put it. It is a part of teaching that one know how to surmount emergencies, such as what Mrs. Hope mentioned when she was here. Every teacher has to face situations like these, and if they happen in the demonstration session, with an experienced teacher coping with them, it helps the observer to see how they can be handled. I think we learn by negative as well as by positive factors."

"Are there laboratory schools for the age groups Bert and I teach?" Bruz asked, with interest.

"Yes," Mr. Johnson answered. "You should plan to go to one. It will not only provide a way to see a well-conducted class in action, but also act as a measuring rod against which you can measure your own teaching."

Norma Newcomb was glancing back over her notes. "Mr. Johnson," she said, "I have pages of notes taken from our discussions here, and I for one will miss our sessions. I feel charged with interest and enthusiasm, which will last for some time. However, I know I will need to get recharged as time goes on; would you give some suggestions on how to do this?"

"A teacher needs to grow," Mr. Johnson replied, "and this is the final point which I would leave with you as our sessions end. A teacher needs to do **The teacher's** continual reading and study. You al-**need for growth** ready have our class text, which you ought to reread from time to time. In addition, you have seen the books and magazines which I have had here on the browsing table, and you have Mrs. Hope's list. Read books such as these, along with the religious education magazines of your denomination. Articles in the popular press will often provide material on the problems of your age group, as well as up-to-date data on subjects like the Holy Land. A teacher should have access to a good Bible encyclopedia, a concordance, and a commentary; he should be constantly seeking to improve his understanding of the Bible.

"But more than this, a teacher needs to grow spiritually. This means consistent Bible study, devotional reading, fellowship with others in the Christian faith, and public worship. Christian teaching is a vocation so great that it demands all that one has in talent, ability, energy, and consecration." He opened his Bible and reread the verses from Ephesians 4 which Frances Lane had diagrammed weeks before:

And his gifts were that some should be apostles, some prophets, some evangelists, some pastors and teachers, for the equipment of the saints, for the work of ministry, for building up the body of Christ, until we all attain to the unity of the faith and of the knowledge of the Son of God, to mature manhood, to the measure of the stature of the fulness of Christ; so that we may no longer be children, tossed to and fro and carried about with every wind of doctrine, by the cunning of men, by their craftiness in deceitful wiles. Rather, speaking the truth in love, we are to grow up in every way into him who is the head, into Christ, from whom the whole body, joined and knit together by every joint with which it is supplied, when each part is working properly, makes bodily growth and upbuilds itself in love.

Mr. Johnson closed his Bible, bowed his head, and said, "Let us pray. . . ."

Mr. Johnson was the last to leave the leadership classroom. Still ringing in his ears were Kate Powell's glowing words: "This class has been *so* interesting, Mr. Johnson! I've enjoyed every session." But he recalled similar tributes which he had received in the past, and experience told him to weigh Kate's remarks against the real issue: How much will her teaching improve?

Before leaving, Bert Smith had shaken hands and said simply, "Good-bye, Mr. Johnson." Mr. Johnson asked himself, "Will the adult class meeting in the Tower Room have better teaching because Bert Smith has attended this class?" He recalled Bert's remark about letting his class ask questions at the end of the lecture; perhaps Bert had caught a glimmer of what the leadership class was trying to do?

His thoughts turned to Bruz. Bruz reminded him of the parable of the soils which Jesus told. He seemed so enthusiastic, but an added assignment at college could quickly stifle his plans for better preparation for his church school class.

In Mary Bliss, there were faint signs of stirring; perhaps a little growth might result. With Norma Newcomb, Ralph Moody, and Frances Lane he felt real progress had been made. The doors had been opened and they had seemingly caught a vision of what lay beyond. How far would they go? He had no answer. The answer lay with them. "O Lord," he prayed, "teach them, and teach *me*, to teach!"

STUDY QUESTIONS

1. Plan an *objective* test and an *essay* test for your church school class. Compare and contrast the expected outcomes.
2. Prepare ten review questions to be used orally with a class.
3. Face up to the alibis which you have used to explain failures within your teaching. How many times could the failure be credited to you as teacher?
4. Write a full report of a class session, recording it in complete detail. Evaluate the plus and minus aspects.
5. Serve as an observer within a class, diagramming the participation of the members.
6. Work out a study schedule which you could use to insure personal growth as a teacher. Include plans for Bible study and devotions, as well as the study of psychology and teaching methods.

BIBLIOGRAPHY

Departmental Books on Methods

The departmental teaching manuals listed below provide practical helps for teachers and leaders concerning needs and characteristics, how pupils learn, the place of the objective in teaching, use of the Bible and curriculum, and various methods of teaching appropriate to each departmental age group. All are published by Judson Press, Valley Forge, Pa.

Teaching Kindergarten Children, Lois Horton Young

Teaching Middlers, Dorothy L. Molan

Teaching Older Youth, Vincie Alessi and Forrest B. Fordham

Divisional Books on Methods

Anderson, Phoebe M., *Living and Learning in the Church School* (Philadelphia: United Church Press, 1965). This book stresses the importance of a person's being identified with a group—especially the Christian community—and the way in which a teacher strives to bring about this relationship.

Hathaway, Lulu, *Partners in Teaching Older Children* (Valley Forge: Judson Press, 1971).

Hemphill, Martha Locke, *Partners in Teaching Young Children* (Valley Forge: Judson Press, 1972).

Isham, Linda, *On Behalf of Children* (Valley Forge: Judson Press, 1975).

Young, Lois Horton, *Dimensions for Happening* (Valley Forge: Judson Press, 1971).

Other Books

Ban, Joseph D., *Education for Change* (Valley Forge: The Judson Press, 1968). A challenging discussion of many changes occurring in our society with biblical resources for understanding them and the kind of teaching ministry which enables Christians to deal with such changes.

Day, LeRoy J., *Dynamic Christian Fellowship* (Valley Forge: The Judson Press, 1960). Deals with small groups in the church and how they may become redemptive fellowships. Makes use of the newer understandings from theology and the social sciences and the way these affect group life. (Major Revision, 1968)

Howe, Reuel L., *The Miracle of Dialogue* (New York: The Seabury Press, Inc., 1963). An exciting story of dialogue as the principle of effective communication in personal relationships.

Leypoldt, Martha M., *40 Ways to Teach in Groups* (Valley Forge: The Judson Press, 1967). A practical guidebook for persons with leadership responsibilities in groups of adults or youth.

Sherrill, Lewis Joseph, *The Gift of Power* (New York: The Macmillan Company, 1955). The thesis of the book is the gift of spiritual power which the Christian religion teaches, "the power to become"—a self that can cope with itself and with the life situations in a modern society.

Snyder, Ross, *On Becoming Human* (Nashville: Abingdon Press, 1967). An educator talks about "discovering yourself and your life world."